Praise for
Never Get a "Real" Job

"This kick-ass book will save you from a kiss-ass job. For best results, read it from your cubicle—and then start planning your farewell trip to the boss's office."

—Chris Guillebeau,
author of *The Art of Non-Conformity*

"It's never too late to become what you could have been . . . this book will get you started!"

—Elliott Bisnow, founder,
Summit Series Conferences

"Scott Gerber is a straight shooter who tells it like it is. *Never Get a "Real" Job* is the Gen Y wake-up call. It's the end of fun and games; time to get a handle on reality. Scott gives solid advice for someone who's buried the 9-to-5, underemployed, or unemployed. If you aren't buying this book for your kids, buy it for yourself."

—Matt Wilson, cofounder, Under30CEO.com

"If you're in search of a wake-up call from your disheveled and sedentary lifestyle, read this book. Scott slaps arrogance, ignorance, and mainstream theory directly in the face with dose after dose of real-world practicality."

—Gary Whitehill,
founder of New York Entrepreneur
Week (NYEW) and The Relentless Foundation

"Every high school senior should be handed this book along with his or her diploma as they cross the graduation stage. Through a skillfully crafted combination of humor, practical advice, and in-your-face wake-up calls, Scott Gerber makes a rock solid case for why, in today's world, the old advice of 'Get good grades, go to college, and get a good job' is outdated and impractical, and how it's not just possible, but highly advisable, to *Never Get a "Real" Job!*"

—**Adam Toren, cofounder and CEO,
YoungEntrepreneur.com; and
coauthor of *Kidpreneurs***

"This book IS NOT for the happily employed, or eager to be employed. If you are, it will either offend you, depress you, or make you want to quit. 'Be afraid, be very afraid,' as Scott says here. But, for all those who have an itchy feeling about the idea of taking a job to merely pay the bills, this book is your savior. *Never Get a "Real" Job* totally personifies the wild ride that is entrepreneurship: It's raw, real, sobering, shocking, making you laugh, cry, curse . . . all while reassuring you that you'd never want to do anything else with your life. It's a frank, candid, in-your-face, no-holds-barred book for the antiemployment types. And there are plenty of those out there. You may be one of them. If you are, *Never Get a "Real" Job* is definitely for you."

—**Jennifer Kushell, founder of YSN.com,
Your Success Network; and author of the
New York Times best-seller, *Secrets of
the Young & Successful***

"I could never hold a 'real' job. If you can't either, read Scott Gerber's new book about how to take control of your own future as a small business owner. You won't always enjoy the ride, but it will be exhilarating!"

—**Barry Moltz,
author of *You Need to Be a Little Crazy***

NEVER
GET A
"REAL"
JOB

NEVER GET A " REAL " JOB

HOW TO **DUMP** YOUR BOSS, **BUILD** A BUSINESS, AND **NOT GO BROKE**

SCOTT GERBER

WILEY

John Wiley & Sons, Inc.

Published by John Wiley & Sons, Inc., Hoboken, New Jersey.
Published simultaneously in Canada.

For general information on our other products and services or for technical support,
please contact our Customer Care Department within the United States at (800)
762-2974, outside the United States at (317) 572-3993 or fax (317) 572-4002.

Wiley also publishes its books in a variety of electronic formats. Some content that
appears in print may not be available in electronic books. For more information about
Wiley products, visit our web site at www.wiley.com.

Library of Congress Cataloging-in-Publication Data:

Gerber, Scott, 1983-
   Never get a "real" job : how to dump your boss, build a business, and not go broke /
Scott Gerber.
      p. cm.
   ISBN 978-0-470-64386-0 (cloth)
   ISBN 978-0-470-92547-8 (ebk)
   ISBN 978-0-470-92548-5 (ebk)
   ISBN 978-0-470-92549-2 (ebk)
   1. Entrepreneurship. 2. Self-employed. 3. New business enterprises. 4. Small
business. 5. Success in business. I. Title.
   HB615.G48 2010
   658.1'1—dc22   2010024730

Printed in the United States of America

10 9 8 7 6 5 4 3 2 1

This book is dedicated to the death of the "real" job.

Die, you miserable bastard.

CONTENTS

ACKNOWLEDGMENTS

I've poured every ounce of blood, sweat, and tears I could muster into *Never Get a "Real" Job*. It's my hope that this book gives you the strength, practical knowledge, and swift kick in the ass you need to avoid unemployment or underemployment, or quit lousy, life-draining 9-to-5s once and for all. May it give you the sense of purpose and perspective you need to kick your boss to the curb and never look back.

Before I shed light on the arduous, yet rewarding journey that lies ahead, I'd like to take a moment to thank the many people who have made *Never Get a "Real" Job* possible. My editorial team was simply top notch. I have never simultaneously loved and hated a group of people as much as the great folks who stood behind me during this grueling process.

To my partner in crime/book and *Entrepreneur* magazine editor, Kimberlee Morrison: Thank you for jumping on board the "Death to the 'Real' Job Express" with me. Your guidance, support, and no-holds-barred editorial approach played an instrumental role in transforming this book from mere words on a page to hardcore advice worth reading. You're one tough cookie, and I love you for it.

Partnering with John Wiley & Sons, Inc., on *Never Get a "Real" Job* was without a doubt the right move. My book editor Dan Ambrosio helped steer this book's content in the right direction from the very beginning. If it weren't for him, I might not have written this book in the first place. Thanks for believing in me, pal. I look forward to a long and prosperous collaboration.

Many thanks to my friends, colleagues, and loved ones who read and reviewed countless drafts and kept me from losing my mind during my quest to reach the Holy Grail of 60,000-plus words: Tana Pierce (the love of my life), Stephen Gnoza, Michael Volpe, Adam Steinhaus, Rachel Cohn, Geoff Glisson, Tyler Cohn, Jenny Winters, Julia Monti, Adam Biren, and Ron Adler. The panel's mix of "real" job loyalists, aspiring small business owners, and hard-liner entrepreneurs made for great debates and insightful exchanges that I won't soon forget.

To Amy Cosper and all of the other great folks at *Entrepreneur* magazine: Thank you for giving me my start as a writer and columnist. It's been one of the greatest privileges of my life to connect with hundreds of thousands of entrepreneurs around the world.

I'm extremely fortunate to have such an amazing bunch of mentors and colleagues in my corner who motivate me to kick ass and take names every day: Rosalind Resnick, Ed Droste, Craig Spierer, John Bellaud, Ron Mannanice, Sharon Badal, Jeff Sloan, Scott Talarico, Robert King, Michael Sinensky, Charlie Stettler, Domenic Rom, Michael Simmons, and Donna Fenn. I thank you all for your continued support of my entrepreneurial ambitions. I also want to shout out all of the great organizations that promoted *Never Get a "Real" Job* while it was being written: Entrepreneur.com, About.com, Extreme Entrepreneurship Tour, Mixergy.com, BusinessInsider.com, Young & Successful, YoungUpstarts.com, SuccessCircuit.com, and Under30CEO.com.

Finally, to my mom and dad, Ellen and Kevin: Thanks for supporting and loving me every step of the way. I know it's not easy to have a son who likes to live on the edge, but you've stayed by my side through thick and thin. For that I am truly grateful. Sure, you guys swear by "real" jobs and have tried to get me to do the same time and time again, but I love you anyway.

FOREWORD

I started my first business when I was 16 years old. Being an entrepreneur has completely changed my life for the better. Simply put, it is the single best professional decision I've ever made.

Over years of hard work, I've written a best-selling book, *The Student Success Manifesto*, spoken to tens of thousands of fellow Generation Yers, built a successful business that promotes entrepreneurship on college campuses called The Extreme Entrepreneurship Tour, and been featured in national media that I only dreamed of.

However, what many people don't know is that I had over $40,000 in credit card debt at my lowest point and had to constantly hear my mom ask me when I was going to get a "real" job.

When I was first getting started, none of my friends had any idea what entrepreneurship was. I can remember the stress of pursuing a vision that I felt I saw clearly, but that no one else could see. I questioned myself constantly about whether or not I was doing the right things. But, I kept on going, and in the end it all paid off. Not because of luck, but because I actually learned how to run a business. I only wish that *Never Get a "Real" Job* had been written when I was getting started so I could have learned from Scott's mistakes instead of my own.

Today's twenty-something-year-olds are experiencing the reality of this book even as I write this foreword. After nearly two decades of schooling (with lots of student debt) in preparation for the "real world," a large percentage of today's young people are moving back in with their parents, taking low-paying jobs that they could have done in grade school, or going on to further education in hopes that there might be a job waiting for them once they graduate. (Good luck!) The reality is that we're all experiencing more of a sign of times to come than of a passing recession. In tomorrow's world, being an entrepreneur will be a requirement for success. If Generation Y adopts this mind-set, I believe it will create a new level of prosperity that we have never seen. However, if it doesn't, I fear that Generation Y will become the 'lost' generation.

Never Get a "Real" Job is a timely book that needed to be written and Scott Gerber is the perfect person to write it. Scott is part of his audience, and he's successfully done what he's asking his readers to do. He has an entertaining style, which makes the book a page-turner.

The old path of going to the "right" school, getting good grades, and going right into your dream job is broken! Which is why this book should be required reading for every college student and twenty-somethings—because it gives people a new, clear path and shows them how to go from where they are to achieving their personal and career goals. Scott provides a solution that he himself recently navigated through. Instead of the typical narrative from other business books: "I'm super successful and twenty years ago when I was in your position, here's what I did," Scott's narrative is more authentic, relatable, and therefore, easier and more effective to apply. He is still in his twenties and very recently in the same exact position as his readers. He admits that he doesn't yet own the Ferrari, yet his success is extremely impressive and inspiring nonetheless.

Never Get a "Real" Job is also very realistic, pulls no punches, and is perfect for the times we're in. It doesn't provide the rosy perspective of: "If you become an entrepreneur, money will take care of itself and you'll be able to live happily ever after." Instead, it warns you about the misconceptions of entrepreneurship and provides a systematic, three-stage approach to minimize your risk and get money in your pocket as soon as possible.

In the end, this book is a great wake up call for both parents and young people. Scott warns parents that the "go to school, get good grades, and get a good job" mantra is broken. At the same time, he doesn't simply let young people off the hook. He shares that to be successful will require a ton of hard work over time, learning new skills, and constantly going outside your comfort zone.

I guarantee that if you follow Scott's advice, your success will not be a question of if; it will be a question of when.

This book and Scott's highly trafficked youth entrepreneurship columns are just the start of the "Never Get a 'Real' Job movement," and I'm honored that my organization is a part of it.

— Michael Simmons,
Founder of the Extreme Entrepreneurship Tour

INTRODUCTION

NEVER GET A "REAL" JOB

"Scott, when are you going to get a *real* job?"

With those words, my mother had decided to bring up *the* question for what seemed like the millionth time—a question that had become the dreaded, bane-of-my-existence conversation starter, one that felt like root canal surgery without the Novocain every time I heard it. Even though I had fought hard to win this discussion countless times before, she simply wouldn't let the topic die.

Being one year out of an expensive university without a "real" job to show for it gave my steady-paycheck, benefits-loving, schoolteacher mother heart palpitations. Granted, I wasn't making much money at the time—but I certainly wasn't living on the streets begging for change, either. My start-up company was generating a modest income—comparable to most entry-level positions—and was enabling me to feed myself, pay my rent, and socialize like any other normal twenty-something-year-old. And although I was busting my ass, hustling my way into pitch meetings with Fortune 500 companies, every time I heard my name in the same sentence with the phrase "real" job—which, according to my mother, meant one with a specific title in which I worked for someone else—well, it was almost as if none of my hard work mattered.

Fear of deviation from the straight-arrow path drove my mother to constantly ask this question of me. And the only way she could calm her fears was to try to scare the hell out of me and to point out why my life choices were unequivocally flawed.

"One day you're going to have a family. How are you going to support them? You'll want a nice house. You'll have to pay a mortgage," she cautioned frequently.

The tone of this discussion changed regularly, usually shifting between loud and louder. However, the main points were always consistent:

"What are you doing with your life?"

"Why did I send you to college?"

"How do you plan to make a living?"

Frustrated and standing my ground, we'd begin the big debate.

"I know what I'm doing," I would reply. "Just because I don't work 9-to-5 like you doesn't mean I'm not making a living."

She'd respond with an apples-to-oranges comparison.

"Your friends are all moving forward in their lives. They all have good jobs and are building their careers. I don't understand why you can't do the same."

I'd throw in some sharp-tongued sarcastic comment criticizing her values.

"You taught me to be a leader, not a follower. Didn't you? Or was that only meant to be applied to every *other* aspect of my life?"

My mother would inevitably try to end the debate with an existential-sounding proverb of her own design meant to illuminate my foolish train of thought.

"You don't want to wake up one day and see that life has passed you by, do you?"

But it never ended there.

This argument was a test of wills; it could go on for five minutes, or five hours. But after all of the pointless back-and-forth banter and skyrocketing blood pressure, the exchange only resulted in a stalemate—and fueled similar debates later.

There is a good reason that becoming an entrepreneur feels so natural to so many of us. Whether they realize it or not—and as I pointed out to my mother during these trying discussions—our parents and our teachers encouraged us to be that way. Years of lauding and back-patting ingrained in us the notion that we could conquer the world. Ironically, what our mentors neglected to teach us was how to actually *live* that lifestyle. And the thought of us *not* getting a job terrifies them. Why? Because our parents learned from our grandparents that a job—preferably a "safe" one, with benefits and a pension—was necessary for survival.

But while our parents and teachers may have felt comforted by this security, rarely was it what they actually *wanted* from their careers. Naturally, they wanted us to pursue our dreams at all costs—sometimes even to the point of risking poverty to put us through college. The problem is that they didn't know truly how to help us get there; and if they didn't know how to survive as entrepreneurs themselves, then how could they teach *us* to avoid getting a "real" job? They couldn't; so we didn't learn. And our education system doesn't fill in that gap. In fact, it's meant to teach us to be employees. So when we graduate, we're made to believe that our choices are to get a "real" job—or to hit the highway.

Rather than chalk my mother's encouragement up as another bedtime story, I chose the highway—and set out to learn the practical skills and tricks necessary to become what she dreamed I would be. These are the lessons I will now teach you.

WHO NEEDS THE 9-TO-5?

The mere thought of living the conventional 9-to-5 life plan—creating wealth for "The Man" instead of for myself—made me want to reach simultaneously for a bottle of Xanax and vodka. Cubicle farms, incompetent bosses, strict dress codes, and inane corporate acronyms crammed into a potentially 50- to 60-hour workweek that was out of my control—in exchange for a paycheck that barely covered expenses—it all sounded like torture. And it wasn't for me. So I simply made up my mind that I was never going to get a "real" job. I'd find a way to make it on my own and create a life of my own design.

I just needed to figure out how the hell to do that.

I took a trip to the local bookstore during my sophomore year of college to find some material written by entrepreneurial peers who could offer me practical insights. After hours upon hours of reading book jackets and tables of contents, the sheer volume of redundant business-plan books and mundane start-up how-to guides overwhelmed me. There were countless books promising quick fixes and instant millions. There were dense dissertations packed with MBA jargon from hoity-toity academic theorists; more than a fair share of war story autobiographies from famous rock star entrepreneurs; and boatloads of overly glamorized soft covers that made entrepreneurship sound as if readers were guaranteed success if they just "set their minds to it."

There wasn't, however, a single, practical book written by a twenty-something-year-old with whom I could identify. Not one book in the entire store by a down-to-earth, Generation Y business owner who had turned the nothing they started with into something they wanted.

I didn't want to learn to incorporate a business or write a business plan; this was hardly insider information, and could be found almost anywhere online anyway. I wanted solid, real-life advice from a peer who understood where I was and what I needed to do to build a business—not just a theoretical plan on paper. With the hope that my assumptions were wrong—and the feeling that I had to buy *something* to get myself on track—I purchased a few titles.

Sadly, I *wasn't* wrong. And I ended up $75.65 poorer as a result.

Most of the books I bought were repetitive and wholly unrealistic for aspiring entrepreneurs. I began to wonder if any of these so-called business experts had ever even met a college student, recent grad, or young person looking to start his or her own business before. Ask friends and family for start-up capital? The author might as well have said, "Good luck, but if daddy doesn't have deep pockets, don't even bother. Get a 'real' job, punk." Apply for bank loans and credit lines to gain access to operating capital? Sure, because so many of us have outstanding credit and have already paid off all of our debts and student loans. Yeah, right.

I might not have had a pot to piss in, but I sure as hell wasn't about to quit because some blowhard authors had penned one-size-fits-all approaches to starting a business in exchange for an advance check from a publisher and an expert credential to headline their blogs.

No matter. Nothing was going to stop me from fulfilling the promise I had made to myself—not even being clueless about how to start a business.

With barely a dollar to my name and no resources to guide me, I did what I thought any half-cocked, passionate, ambitious, impulse-driven know-it-all would do: I got started and figured it out for myself. Crazy? Perhaps. But in the end, my decision and subsequent hard work paid off tenfold. Sure, there were nights I went hungry and days I nearly starved. But as the months and years passed, I found ways to feed myself quite well—all without a suitable guidebook. Fortunately, you won't have to face the same situation; it's a problem I've now remedied for you with *Never Get a "Real" Job*.

I KNOW YOU

Let me be clear: I don't have millions of dollars in the bank, six-figure sports cars, or gold-plated yachts. I'm not the product of a wealthy family or a storied entrepreneurial heritage; nor am I the outcome of an accredited business school. In fact, I graduated from a film school where I never attended a single business or mathematics class.

So why should you listen to what I have to say? After all, who am I to tell you how to build a successful business?

Because I know what it's like to have to move back in with your parents and how depressing it is to have shrinking bank accounts and mounting debts. I know what's in store for you. I know what you think is going to happen versus what will actually happen.

I understand you, because I *am* you.

I was where you are right now—confused, eager, antsy, disappointed, scared, unfulfilled, and ready for something more; and not 30 years ago, either. Most importantly, my journey—and its results—are proof that *anyone* has the ability to survive, thrive, and make the seemingly impossible happen—all without ever needing to get a "real" job.

Since I became an entrepreneur, I've built several successful companies, and others that didn't last more than three months. I've worked alongside both smart partners and idiots. I've made a lot of money—but I've failed more times than I've succeeded. Through it all, I've always been my own boss; I've never worked for "The Man," and I've never gone bankrupt. Both my successes and failures have prompted me to develop new ways of thinking about business. I've created business planning, bootstrapping, and sales and marketing methodologies that have enabled me to build a steady and sustainable lifestyle, supported by a healthy six-figure income. I've shared my strategies with tens of thousands of aspiring entrepreneurs through my syndicated *Entrepreneur* column—and will now share them with you in this book.

WHAT YOU CAN EXPECT TO GET FROM THIS BOOK

Let's get a few things straight at the outset. I don't have any magic formulas for raising capital or get-rich-quick schemes. If you're looking for cutesy gimmicks and paperwork exercises, then look elsewhere. If you're shopping for a miracle cure or infomercial-style promises that will get you from zero to hero in a week, allow me to offer you some free advice: your ideals are totally unrealistic, and unless you change your mind-set, you're hopeless. You can't lose 50 pounds in one week by sitting stationary in a chair with a machine strapped around your gut; and you can't build a successful, lucrative, and sustainable business overnight.

Unlike many other start-up guide books that offer you a few tips that might help you make a quick buck, the multifaceted approach to entrepreneurship I present to you here includes a full attack on your lifestyle. It presents logic that will challenge you mentally and emotionally, and asks you to make many tough choices, the outcomes of which will affect every facet of your life. All of this is done for a single purpose: To train you to generate immediate income to support yourself and build a business—whether you have a budget or not a single dollar to your name.

This book helps you to become a person who sees no limits, doesn't believe in boundaries, and won't take no for an answer. It helps you become a person who balks at the 9-to-5 system that conditions us to be dependent, and someone who stays the course even when independence is hard—or damn near impossible. This book helps you become a person unafraid to fail even when conventional wisdom would say to play it safe. Above all, it will teach you that entrepreneurship isn't just about what you know, what you do well, or even who you know—but rather, whether you can execute effectively and *make things happen*. Some people get it; most people don't. This book teaches you how to get it.

ALL ABOARD THE DEATH TO THE "REAL" JOB EXPRESS!

Whether you're wasting away in a cubicle wanting to climb the tallest clock tower, feverishly mailing out resumes, praying you'll get a "real" job to help you start paying down college loans, or a student who's terrified to graduate to the real world to a position as an underemployed grunt—here is my challenge to you: Give yourself the opportunity to take control of your own destiny, walk on your own two feet, and fail or succeed on your own terms.

Accept my challenge? Good.

Welcome aboard the Death to the "Real" Job Express—a one-way ticket to the new and self-sufficient you. I'll be your conductor.

The coddling is over. I'm not going to handle you with kid gloves or sugarcoat anything. If that's the sort of education you're looking for, apply to an MBA program. I didn't write this book to tell you how special you are—because, to be quite honest, you're not. You're not a delicate flower or a ray of sunshine. I don't care about your college degree, your pedigree, or how much you have in the bank—and guess what? Neither does the rest of the world. I'm here to tell it like it *really* is. Not like you wish it was or thought it was going to be, and certainly not like your parents, professors, and MTV told you it would be. I plan to treat you and your start-up the same way the real world will—and that is to say, not favorably.

Now, forget everything you thought you knew to be true. Leave your preconceived notions about the "real" job at the door, and tune out your parents, professors, and the pundits. It isn't going to be easy—but together, we're going to deconstruct you, build a solid foundation, and help you to rebuild your ideal entrepreneurial self that will be prepared to avoid the dreaded 9-to-5 lifestyle.

Now, hop on board. Next stop: Learning to become the self-employed business owner you were meant to be.

PART I

THE BREAKDOWN

1

EVERYONE POOPS. YOURS ISN'T SPECIAL

When our parents came of age in the 1950s, 1960s, and 1970s, working for "The Man" was the only game in town. Our grandparents—mostly members of the Great Depression generations for whom jobs were considered luxuries—reinforced the ideas that getting a job and working hard were essential to building a sustainable living.

Thus, the mantra was born: Work hard, get good grades, go to college, and get a job.

Before we were even born, our parents fantasized about what we would be when we grew up. They wanted things to be better for us, but in a much different way than their parents had planned for them. There was a generational divide here: To our grandparents, getting a job was a matter of survival. But our parents wanted more than survival for us—they wanted us to find our dream job and thrive. We couldn't just get *any* job—they had much bigger ideas for us. They wanted us to find a cure for a disease, write the next great American novel, or become president of the United States. The possibilities seemed endless. Their expectations ran wild and knew no bounds. Before the doctor even cut our umbilical cords, we were already winners who were destined to surpass their wildest dreams—even though they had no idea what that meant or how we could even begin to make their dreams a reality.

And, then the big day arrived. You might have entered the world as an 8-pound ton-of-fun with a face that scared off the family dog, but it didn't matter. The moment you left the womb, you were a special, perfect, one-in-a-million diamond-in-the-rough who would one day perform open-heart surgery blindfolded, while climbing Everest.

From that day forward, the world revolved around your every action. You giggled, and your parents thought it was brilliant. You rolled over, and you were amazing. When you walked, they told everyone who would listen how incredible you were. You mumbled some incoherent iteration of "mom" or "dad" that sounded more like "bus stop"—and it was *life changing*. Relatives would even line up to clean your diaper just to get a whiff of your majestic, rosy fragranced poop.

And the adoration didn't end at infancy.

It was time to call the NBA when you *almost* hit that foul shot during your fourth-grade basketball scrimmage. Graduating from middle school was a crowning achievement. And when you made your singing debut in the high school musical's background ensemble, your parents swore that you were on your way to Broadway.

For years, your parents, teachers, and MTV blew smoke up your ass at every turn. You were showered with undeserved accolades, encouraged to aspire to unrealistic goals, and praised for exaggerated achievements. You were the unwitting victim of a coddling culture fated to screw up your perception of reality.

No matter how pathetic the award or how asinine the proverb, you bought into it all, hook, line, and sinker. You were so busy riding the Everyone-Is-a-Winner bandwagon that you failed to realize that you were being rewarded for mediocrity—or worse, out of pity. Your parents put you on a teetering pedestal, instead of providing you a strong and realistic foundation for the rest of your life. Encouraging you to aim high is one thing, but by keeping you from feeling the sting of failure—and not allowing you space to fend for yourself independently—your parents, teachers, and coaches unknowingly set you up to be a weak, ineffectual person, unprepared for adulthood.

COLLEGE: THE DRUNKEN ROAD TO EASY STREET

From your time in the cradle, up to high school graduation, you were likely force-fed everything from *Sesame Street* to SAT prep courses. You were pushed to read faster, be smarter, and raise your GPA in the hopes that one day you'd be accepted into a top-rated college—and that would set you up for life.

But rather than instilling the desire to pursue a "real" job, college taught you to hate them. Most professors were open-minded thought leaders who encouraged discussion. Unlike the mandated dress codes in primary and secondary schools, college promoted a sense of individuality and expression. No one dictated where or how you worked, as long as you got the work done. Cheating or achieving grades so low that teachers began to question whether you had a pulse were two of very few reasons you might be expelled—which were better odds than hoping for job security.

When you did manage to find the time to pay attention or even make it to class, you probably realized that your classes weren't offering you the critical skills necessary for the real world. College courses seemed to train you for the same mythical dream job your parents desired for you. There were no lectures on corporate hierarchy, filing documents, or answering phones. When you weren't wasting time taking classes that were about as useful as a screen door on a submarine, you were receiving a high-level education that taught you how to do your eventual employer's job, not the remedial tasks of his entry-level assistant. Simply put, you were told *what* to think—not *how* to think.

Instead of breaking free from the system and taking control of your own life, you took the easy road. You decided to allow your perception of reality to remain warped, because you knew you had a reward just waiting to be cashed in. Your BS in BS was your meal ticket to superior job placement and untold riches.

Or so you thought.

DUDE, WHERE'S MY DREAM JOB?

The years passed by so fast that before you knew it, you were finishing up your senior year of college. In a few short months you'd be pants-less, wearing a cap and gown, accepting a six-figure sheet of oak tag, and finding yourself one step closer to retirement by thirty. All of the B− term papers and drunken debauchery was finally going to pay off. It was time to get paid!

You typed up your resume in 12-point Times New Roman with your name centered at the top in bold caps. You grossly exaggerated your internship experience and gave yourself the title of VP of Operations, Marketing, and Accounting. You printed the document on 110-pound scented yellow stationery and—along with your formulaic cover letter—proudly handed the completed package to your career development counselor for her seal of approval. I'm sure there was a tear in his or her eye. You then proceeded to send resumes to all of the best employers you could find on the Web. The excitement was palpable. It was time to accept your dream job.

A few weeks went by, and you didn't hear anything—but you didn't let that scare you. You had an *accredited* degree. But still, where was the harm in hedging your bets? So you sent out 10 more resumes.

A few more weeks passed. No responses.

No problem, though, right? It was only a matter of time before someone contacted you to schedule an interview. After all, you followed your life plan to the *decimal.* You got good grades, and were accepted into college—now the next step was to get the job of your dreams. Right? But just to be sure, you sent out a few more resumes. Not too many. Just 75 or so . . . you know, to be on the safe side.

There's a good possibility that if you graduated several years ago, you applied for a bunch of corporate gigs and still haven't heard back from any employers. You're not alone. Juan Somavia, the Director-General of the UN International Labour

Organization, has recently announced that global youth unemployment has hit its highest levels ever, with 81 million young people unemployed worldwide. According to a 2009 National Association of Colleges and Employers study, 80 percent of college graduates who were looking for jobs couldn't find one. The Economic Policy Institute recently announced that the class of 2010 faces the worse job market in a generation, with the Bureau of Labor Statistics putting unemployment among 19- to 24-year-olds over 15 percent. Even more disturbing is the recent study by the Pew Research Center indicating that nearly 40 percent of all 18- to 29-year-olds have either been unemployed or underemployed at some point since December 2007.

If you did hear from a potential employer, there's a fairly good chance you were denied a position because you were either underqualified for the jobs you wanted or overqualified for the jobs you applied for "just to make ends meet." It didn't matter if you had a degree in electrical engineering—you'd be lucky to get an executive assistant gig at a corporate event planning company, if you got a job at all.

But there *is* a silver lining. You're now a card-carrying member of the Boomerang Club: The first generation in history to attend college only to move back in with dear old mom and dad afterward because you're broke, unemployed, and in debt up to your eyeballs.

Hooray for living the dream!

I'm sure this is *exactly* how you envisioned your postcollegiate life.

WELCOME TO YOUR "REAL" JOB, MR. JANITOR

Maybe you were "fortunate" and did manage to land a job after college. However, chances are that whatever you're currently doing was not your first choice. It's probably not even your 10th or 20th choice. Heck, it's probably not even your *100th* choice. Instead of being hired as the vice president of fashion design at Ralph Lauren, you most likely accepted a receptionist gig at Joey Fatayat's Mortuary where the motto "You Kill 'Em, We Chill 'Em" is proudly displayed on a neon sign in the parking lot. (I'm sure they have a *wonderful* health insurance plan.)

And if, by some miracle, you were lucky enough to get a job in your chosen field, then you're most likely grinding it out as an underappreciated, underpaid, underemployed, bottom-of-the-food-chain receptionist-barista-gopher, who often gets mistaken for the company intern.

What happened to the dream job that was dangled in front of you like a carrot on a stick for your entire life?

You departed college with the notion that you were regularly going to make life and death decisions and close billion dollar deals over dinner meetings. So how is it, exactly, that you ended up sitting in a cubicle typing up your supervisor's meeting agenda, staring at a slow ticking wall clock, and wondering where it all went wrong? Where was your standing ovation for handing in your work early? Or the certificate for being on time every morning? How about the corner office with a view or the "important" responsibilities?

Where is your "A" for effort?

Claustrophobic cubicles, stale coffee, monotone dress codes, idiot bosses, mind-numbing water cooler debates, migraine-inducing birthday celebrations, infantile office politics, futile reports, repetitive phone answering protocols . . . the only thing stopping you from running down the hallway screaming like a madman is the thought of being forced to attend the human resource department's new multicultural anger management seminar.

Truth be told, whether your collar is blue or white, your "real" job is probably everything you never wanted it to be—and you're not alone. More people than ever are less than pleased with their current positions. In fact, according to a recent study conducted by the Conference Board, 45 percent of Americans hate their jobs, and—perhaps more shocking—73 percent of Americans under the age of 25 hate their jobs. If that many people are so completely miserable doing what they do on a daily basis ... well, doesn't that tell you something about how broken the system is? Despite the encouragement you received (and still receive) to get one, "real" jobs present a problem for the following reasons:

Real jobs offer you a false sense of security. You've been conditioned to believe that a real job will offer you safety and security. However, the truth is that job security no longer exists—and it hasn't for a long time.

Consider the numerous corporations that went bankrupt in the 2000s where the decisions of the few greatly impacted the livelihoods of the many: Enron, Lehman Brothers, Circuit City, Linens 'N Things, General Motors, and so on. The list is frustratingly endless. Forget about gold watches and retirement lunches; in many cases, loyal employees didn't even receive severance or a shred of their decimated retirement savings. And let's not forget about the recession that has forced companies to lay off millions of employees—nearly 1 in 10, in some instances—just to maintain viability ... and has caused the unemployment rate to escalate to levels that haven't been seen since the Great Depression.

Detractors may argue that employees benefit from more security than entrepreneurs do. Yet although entrepreneurs understand the risks they're taking in terms of their financial security, they still maintain total control over its direction. People with "real" jobs have very little—if any—say over financial and job security. The list of factors that can send you packing will only grow as employers continue to perfect their "better, faster, cheaper" philosophy to keep stockholders happy or increase top-level executive pay. There is only one thing that will undoubtedly become more and more commonplace: pink slips.

Real jobs render you powerless. Clueless management. Moronic colleagues. Tedious reports. Unrealistic deadlines.

What do all of these things have in common? It's simple: No one wants or cares about your opinion on *any* of them. Your job is to keep your head down and get whatever needs handling done—no questions asked.

Don't kid yourself. In most instances, you're not a decision maker unless you are *the* decision maker—and chances are, you're scared of whoever this truly is. In fact, according to a research poll conducted by workplace expert and *BusinessWeek* columnist Lynn Taylor, the average U.S. employee spends more than 19 hours each week worrying about what their boss will do or say. That hardly seems productive to the corporate bottom line.

Unlike entrepreneurs who succeed or fail based on their own decisions, employees with "real" jobs must play the roles of obedient cogs in the machine tasked with performing X function Y amount of times to get Z result for the sole benefit of the mother ship. Deviation from the carefully designed corporate agenda dictated from above could result in unforeseen losses—and consequently, the termination of employment. After all, such actions prohibit you from improving the wealth of others and that cannot be tolerated. Mind you, even if you abide by the corporate agenda and there are losses, it still doesn't mean you're guaranteed any sort of safety—or severance. Say good-bye to freedom and hello to a life as a corporate wage slave.

Real jobs overwork and underpay you. A recent study conducted by the National Institute of Occupational Safety and Health found that the average U.S. employee works two months longer than an employee from 1969 for nearly the same salary after inflation adjustments.

So, not only are many people overworked—they're also paid less for working more.

What does this mean to you in dollars and cents? Maybe $35,100 annually; the average salary for 25- to 34-year-olds in the United States according to the July 2010 *BusinessWeek* article "Retirement: Gen Y's Empty Piggy Bank"—a dollar amount that has come to be after falling 19 percent over the last 30 years after adjusting for inflation. For many entry-level employees, the workday doesn't end at 5 PM—and it often includes portions of weekends. So, we'll suppose that between putting out your boss's fires at 10 PM on Fridays and composing reports during football game viewing on Sundays, that your actual workweek is 50 hours long. Breaking down your annual salary, your actual wage is a little more than $13.50 per hour. Now let's include overtime. Oops—I forgot; according to the Department of Labor's overtime rules, you might not even be eligible for overtime! Silly me. And let's not forget about deductions to your paycheck for taxes and social security. So we'll make that more like $10 per hour. After you subtract for your clothing, travel expenses, college debts, and any costs associated with your company benefits package, well, you're lucky if you can afford a night out at the movies.

On the bright side, you do get paid vacation days. Unfortunately, the average U.S. employee only gets around 13 vacation days—well below that of his counterparts in most other industrialized nations (Italy's average is 42, France's is 37, and Canada's is 26). And according to the May 2009 CNN.com article, "Layoff Worries Keep Many from Taking Vacations," 34 percent of Americans don't even use all of their vacation time because they're too afraid of losing their jobs. And although you might be eligible for a raise in a year or so, that's only likely to happen if the corporate bigwigs haven't taken all the profits to buy new vacation homes.

Job-happy stalwarts may claim that being an entrepreneur doesn't guarantee you'll make more money than a salaried employee or work less hours—and they'd be right. However, unlike "real" job employees—who are stuck in predetermined pay grades and boss-dictated work schedules—entrepreneurs benefit directly from every minute they spend on their business and have the ability to earn as much money as their efforts can produce. As companies continue to streamline their processes— and globalization continues sending jobs overseas to cheaper labor markets—employees will find it increasingly more dif- ficult to land a job that's willing to tolerate a more lenient work-life balance or pay them what they truly deserve for a full "40-hour" workweek.

Real jobs don't reward you for excellence. Not only are your wages pathetic—they are also a minuscule fraction of the marked-up prices that your company is charging its clients. Customers may be paying 10 times more than what you're earning, but other than the possibility of a small bonus, do you know what your upside is? Bupkes. Nothing. Zero. Zilch. Zip. Well, except—maybe—a health benefits package (although, according to a Pew Research Study, Gen Y is the least likely generation to receive health benefits, with nearly 40 percent uncovered by any sort of health plan whatsoever). No, the majority of the revenue that you generate goes toward overhead costs and lining the pockets of the senior executives. Did you have any idea that you were such a thoughtful and generous employee?!

In the end, your workweek translates into nothing more than a paycheck and the honor of begging your incorrigible, take-all-of-the-credit boss for an insignificant promotion that may or may not include a measly raise. Sure, you might get an increase in wages or a bonus; however, it's a mere frac- tion of the upside you've produced. Equity? Partner status? Ha! In most companies, those are simply hilarious jokes to tell your fellow disgruntled employees around the water cooler. Your company expects you to give everything you have—and more—without offering you real incentives for the harder work. And even if a company does offer some sort of stock option, accepting it merely renders you that much more dependent on the *only* hand that feeds you, by putting even more of your eggs into a single basket that you're neither holding, nor have a real say in. I'm glad that you trust your CEO with your financial future. I wonder if he feels the same way about you?

Real jobs slowly kill your entrepreneurial ambitions. Real jobs have one mission: to ensure that you keep creating value for employers under the guise of safety, security, and career advancement. Little by little, inch by inch, "real" jobs suck the humanity from you, enticing you to put self-sufficiency on the backburner by luring you deeper into their pockets with promises of bonuses, extra vacation days, and cute-sounding perks like "casual Fridays." Distractions and tasks start to get the better of you and complacency takes over. Before you realize it, you've begun meeting fewer people; your drive dissipates; your ambitions dwindle; and your passions take a back seat to "getting things done." Suddenly, you've been transformed into a hollow shell of yourself, tricked into putting your plans on hold indefinitely—willing to deal with your misery in exchange for the comfort of a paycheck. You're stuck because now you feel like you really can't lose your "real" job. You're doomed because you don't know how to make it on your own or you have nothing to fall back on.

THE BROKEN PROMISE

Face it: The "work hard, get good grades, and go to college to get a good job" philosophy is obsolete and completely irrelevant to our generation. Times have changed. Our mentors wanted us to apply their lessons to the world as they experienced it. They simply assumed that their way of life would continue; they didn't get the memo that they were disconnected, out of touch, and living in a new world where a one-person business armed with an e-mail address and a mobile phone can rival captains of industry. (Actually, it was probably e-mailed to them, and they forgot to call us to ask how to open the attachment.)

Today's job market is virtually nonexistent because of explosive population growth, the overexpansion of educational institutions, and the effects of globalization. There were only a few million students enrolled in U.S. institutions when our parents went to college. There are more than 19 million today—not to mention millions more taking classes part-time or online. Similarly, our parents weren't competing for jobs in a global marketplace when they graduated. Like our grandparents, they mostly worked jobs within their local communities—in a time before the Internet—when local consumption was high and the country still produced its own products. Today, many of us don't graduate from college to seek out local employment; instead, we compete globally for jobs as assistants to assistants who recycle data and produce nothing of real, tangible value.

Bottom line: We were promised more, and expected more as a result. By the time we discovered our dream jobs were imaginary, it was too late. We ended up being forced into an assembly line system known as the "real" job.

There were countless people you encountered along the way who could have explained the ways of the real world to you. But instead, everyone consciously decided to shield you from its harsh realities and fill your head with innumerable motivational sound bites. Your mother told you to "Work hard and you'll go far." Your high school valedictorian inspired you to "Pursue your dreams." MTV proclaimed, "You can do whatever you set your mind to."

But do any of these catch phrases sound remotely applicable to the 9-to-5 lifestyle as we've come to know and experience it today? How many employed recent college grads do you know are "living the dream"? Most aren't even working in their fields of study—*if* they have jobs at all. I'm sure the individual with the $100,000 degree in public relations is thrilled about his position as the resident coffee and copy grunt for an insurance broker.

No one ever said, "Work hard so that you get better placement in the system." Why? Because no one actually wanted you to become a corporate slave; they wanted you to fulfill their delusional expectations. And when their concepts of your dream job didn't materialize out of nowhere, you were told that you needed to get a "real" job. Now you're expected to forget everything you've ever known because you need to pay the bills. But when we can't even get "real" jobs—or the ones we're accepting aren't even in our field—what does that say about the credibility of "the system"?

Contrary to what you may have been told, avoiding climbing the corporate ladder does *not* mean you are doomed to fail in life. *You* define your success in this world—not your parents, mentors, or teachers. They have—or eventually will—let their fears for your security, livelihood, and well-being overshadow the core values they instilled in you. Their values are still right; but their applications of those ideals are outdated, flawed, and no longer apply to your reality.

If you're one of the tens of millions of young people who can't even get their footing on the corporate ladder—let alone climb it—then now isn't the time to actively keep putting your future in someone else's hands by continuing to mail out resumes. Such an action is the equivalent of inserting a quarter into a broken arcade game, losing it to the machine, and popping another quarter in, hoping for a different outcome.

This is not a job market—it is an *opportunity* market.

Stop trying to fight your way into the system—and fight your way around it instead. If you're wasting away at a 9-to-5 job, stop hurting yourself and your future. Paychecks come and go; but wasted time is gone forever. Rather than wasting time, money, and resources on sending out resumes or working dead-end "real" jobs to make ends meet, it's time to refocus your energies on attaining and securing your financial independence.

Never let those around you dismiss your passions and ambitions as a symptom of postcollegiate stress disorder or shrug off your contempt for the system as the ramblings of a disgruntled employee. It's never wrong to want more, so long as you keep both feet on the ground and a level head on your shoulders. With the proper training, attitude, and dedication, you have the power to build a revenue-generating business and rise above the antiquated social conditioning that is the 9-to-5 mentality.

However—if you think that just because mommy and daddy screwed you up that you're entitled to be an entrepreneur—*boy*, have you got another thing coming.

2

No One Cares About You— Unless You *Make* Them Care

"What are you going to be when you grow up?" This is a profound question we're expected to answer at too young of an age, and for all of the wrong reasons.

For example, I knew growing up that I loved the arts. However, I didn't discover my "dream job" until a fateful day in English class during my sophomore year of high school. Our midterm assignment was to do a project about the 1960s. The class was divided into groups, and we were given complete creative flexibility. So rather than construct a cheesy diorama or give some boring oral presentation, my group opted to produce a short film for which I was the director. From that moment on, I was hooked. My calling became evident:

Show business!

Suddenly, I was obsessed with becoming the next great American auteur; the most famous film director Tinsel Town had ever known. I even gave myself a self-important sounding nickname: "Spielgerber."

Sure, I'd yet to direct anything more than a high school play. But I could look you in the eye and tell you with absolute certainty the license plate number of my future Ferrari.

I began to connect with various members of my high school's alumni who I found out had gone on to work in "the business" (that's how Hollywood insiders—and wannabe insiders—refer to it). All of them *claimed* to be directors, producers, or screenplay writers; yet in reality they were production assistants merely *hoping* to fill those positions one day.

I remember thinking to myself I'd never be like those poor schmucks working their way up to the director's chair by slogging it out 25 hours a day as some coffee gopher. I was Scott Gerber—Tour De Force, future star, and guaranteed millionaire. I was destined to direct a big-budget Orwellian masterpiece right out of college and make millions.

Boy, was I a moron.

Or, as my friends would kindly put it, an arrogant, pretentious, unrealistic jackass caught in a self-absorbed fantasy world. They weren't wrong. That was a kind assessment.

It wasn't until years later when I got some real-world experience under my belt that I realized how misguided and delusional I truly was. After deep reflection, I also realized that the only way I'd find success was to rid myself of my irrational ideals.

I wish I could say that I'm an exception, but sadly, this entitled mentality is hardly uncommon in Gen Y. Sure, part of the blame rests with the loved ones who rewarded us with the same shiny plastic medallions for participating in elementary school spelling bees. But truly, most of the blame is our own. We went from being children—helpless victims who were told all along about how great we were—to being adults, conscious of our own mediocrity, patting ourselves on the back for having done nothing.

Our coddled upbringing and fearless attitudes make us willing to take more risks than previous generations. The same outlook also makes us cocky, careless, and, at times, reckless know-it-alls who are under the impression that the world owes us something. Although Gen Y has been referred to as the most entrepreneurial generation in history, we've also been called irrational whiners, cry babies, spoiled brats, gratification whores, fame-seekers, approval junkies, and the entitlement generation.

You know what? We deserve every bit of it.

Why? Because the vast majority of us walk around as if our brilliance and enthusiasm entitle us to fame, fortune, and instant success. Well—that couldn't be a bigger load of crap.

Like alcoholics or drug addicts, the first step to recovery is admitting we have a problem. There are deeply rooted psychological issues that we must get rid of if we are to learn how to take control of our lives and our careers and eventually become successful entrepreneurs. We can continue to live in a fantasy world if we want—but this flawed logic will result in behavioral and emotional traits that are likely to lead us down a one-way road to failure.

Now close your eyes and take a deep breath. You're about to pop the hot-air-filled balloon known as your head.

YOU ARE NOT SPECIAL

I hate to break it to you, but your life is not a reality TV show. And even if it were, no one would watch anyway. Contrary to what you believe, the world does not revolve around you. In fact, it doesn't know or even care that you exist. Yes, you're one in a billion—and not in that egotistical way you're thinking.

You're simply one in a billion. Period. That's it. End of story.

You are not exempt from hard work simply because you have a skill and exist on this planet. Don't convince yourself that you will be able to open doors with a snap of your fingers. Such thinking will lead you on a downward spiral that—as the late Chris Farley said—"ends with you sleeping in a van down by the river, eating a steady diet of government cheese." You're not as important as you think you are. You're just Joe Schmuck, creator of the next widget *you* believe will change people's lives.

With the possible exception of your family and friends, no one will care about your product or your start-up. Unless they are paying customers, their opinions are worthless. There are millions of people—most of whom are bigger, stronger, faster, and smarter than you—who are vying for the same attention from the same prospects. Every one of them is trying to open those same doors, and is spouting the same sales pitches supported by the same inflated, self-proclaimed executive title.

If you want to become an effective and respected leader, you have to stop walking around like you're better than everyone else. You're not. If you believe that all you have to do is tell people how special you are to earn their business, you're starting with a deeply flawed mind-set right out of the gate.

Your McLife—one which has turned you into a lazy, Xbox-addicted couch potato, incapable of long-term survival without Hot Pockets—has fooled you into believing that everything you want can be attained easily and instantaneously. You've been brainwashed into thinking that everything will happen in 30 seconds or less—and that you'll reap great rewards with the most minimal efforts.

Get real! Not everything is microwaveable. Rome wasn't built in a day, and if you think your business will be, you're in for a rude awakening—followed by regular trips to the soup kitchen. Get this instant gratification nonsense out of your head or you'll quit long before your start-up even has the chance to fail.

CLAIMING TO BE A WINNER DOES NOT MAKE YOU ONE

Too many people think they're winners these days. Even the worst of the worst *American Idol* rejects—the ones who couldn't sing on key if a madman was pressing a gun to their puppies' heads—have convinced themselves that they're talented and great.

If everyone is a winner, then I ask you: Where are all of the losers?

Face it: Not everyone gets rewarded with a trophy or a pat on the back. Life is a competition with real winners and losers. Second place is simply one step closer to bankruptcy.

There are concrete reasons why some people sink and others swim. When losers get knocked down, they stay down—but keep talking. When winners get knocked down, they learn from their mistakes and stand up stronger. Losers talk about what they want to do; winners get it done. Losers quit because the race is too hard. Winners hustle across the finish line, no matter what it takes.

YOU'RE BRILLIANT ... SO WHAT?

Here's a joke for you. What's the difference between toilet paper and an MBA in a start-up?

Give up?

One is actually useful.

Congratulations on your perfect SAT score and graduating Magna Cum Laude. I'm sorry to be the bearer of bad news, but no one cares. Don't get me wrong; I'm not saying book smarts aren't important. Who doesn't enjoy participating in a rousing game of Jeopardy every once in a while? But gloating about the A+ you received on your midterm paper detailing the consumer trends in emerging third-world nations will not translate into more revenue for your business.

Yes, you'll need to be able to properly articulate your value proposition and communicate it intelligently to prospective customers and partners. However, to survive in the real world, there is a different set of secret weapons on which you'll need to rely: hustler instincts, the intuition for problem solving, and good old-fashioned perseverance. These traits will enable you to open closed doors, surpass your competitors, and make things happen.

LIFESTYLES OF THE POOR AND VAIN

Be honest. You've undoubtedly daydreamed about owning yachts, Rolexes, mansions, and a Rolls-Royce. There's absolutely nothing wrong with this dream. I still hope to someday drive my Ferrari into the garage of my private 4,000-acre beach resort in Fiji. However, if the only reason you want to become your own boss is so you can live out some MTV *Cribs* fantasy, the only Rolls-Royce you'll ever drive is the one the successful people hire you to chauffeur.

Get your head out of your idealistic *E! True Hollywood Story* ass.

The goal to become rich and famous leads to developing an unrealistic state of mind that will prove detrimental to your decision-making abilities. Indulging in a foolhardy, ego-driven, "going-for-millions" mentality will quickly become a "going-for-broke" gamble that will lead you one step closer to saying, "Would you like fries with that?"

Most business owners never earn millions or bask in the spotlight. Does this mean that most small business owners are *failures*? Absolutely not. For every trendy start-up you hear about Google acquiring for 10 figures, there are hundreds of thousands of successful small businesses you've never heard of that generate a healthy income to support the lifestyle of some smart entrepreneur and his family.

Don't fall for the hype. Not only did the rock star entrepreneurs you've seen and read about in the media work *extremely* hard to make it big, they were also lucky. They were in the right place at the right time, with the right story and the right product or service. I'm not saying that you'll never achieve this level of success, but you'll be better off reorganizing your priorities, resetting your expectations, and setting more realistic goals.

SHUT UP, PINOCCHIO

You have a dormant virus inside of you, and if you don't get the antidote fast, it's only a matter of time before it overtakes your business.

At first, the virus will seem harmless. You might begin by enthusiastically promoting your business idea as a "sure thing" to perfect strangers. Slowly but surely, the Stage 2 symptoms will start to cloud your judgment—and you'll begin introducing yourself to prospective significant others by handing them a business card and saying, "Hi, I'm a CEO." Before you know what hits you, the full bug will manifest itself, causing you to uncontrollably spew irrational, nonsensical verbal diarrhea ad nauseam. Without revenue or a single client, you'll convince yourself that Apple's acquisition of your masterpiece is inevitable—and then it's only a matter of time before you retire to a private island, smoking hand-rolled cigars crafted from $100 bills.

Am I referring to salmonella or mad cow disease? No. I'm talking about the Liar's Disease.

Want to guarantee that no one will trust your abilities or your company? Keep talking out of your ass. There is a fine line between enthusiasm and exaggeration. Don't cross it. Pathological smooth talking or outright lying will cause others to view you as an untrustworthy, arrogant used-car salesperson.

Instead—be authentic. From your clothing to your work ethic, you are sending a message to others with every decision you make. Whether you're a T-shirt-wearing tech-nerd or a super-polished, suit-clad tight ass, be *real*. Own and accept who you are and what you do. Underpromise and overdeliver—not the other way around. Make sure that everything you say is backed up with real, measurable results. A solid track record of high-quality work will sell others on your value much better than any cheap rhetoric.

Walk the walk, or don't talk the talk. Talk isn't just cheap. Sometimes, it can kill your business.

PUT IT ON MY TAB

Remember the good old days when your parents gave you an allowance? Pick up a toy, get a dollar. Do your homework, get a dollar. Say hello to your grandparents, get a dollar, plus some interest to boot from your beloved grandma. Those were the days when money grew on trees.

All those years you received gifts and free money have given you a taste for the finer things in life. You've come to enjoy spending expensive nights out, purchasing lavish toys, and sipping overpriced lattes. Bill? You'll deal with that later! After all, you're not spending real money; you're spending imaginary plastic money, right?

There's only one small problem: You haven't earned it yet!

According to the April 2010 *USA TODAY* article, "Generation Y's steep financial hurdles: Huge debt, no savings," the average Gen Yer owns *more than* 3 credit cards and 20 percent carry more than a $10,000 balance. What the hell do any of us need three interest-accruing credit cards for?

This "pay-for-it-later" mentality needs to stop—right now! Life won't be paying you an allowance—so stop pissing money away as though you have an unlimited surplus. Credit cards and ATM machines aren't spitting money out at you because you're "kind of a big deal." They can quickly become liabilities, preying on your ignorance and immaturity and bleeding you dry—if you let them.

Five Must-Reads That Will Help Get Your Finances in Order

Just because your bank account resembles a low IQ score doesn't mean you can't start a business. The first thing you need to do is to take control of your financial life by ditching your bad habits and creating systems for saving money and increasing your income. These five titles—by some of the smartest personal finance and financial literacy gurus around—can help you get on the right track.

(*continued*)

(*continued*)

1. *Rich Dad Poor Dad* by Robert T. Kiyosaki (RichDad.com) teaches you the essentials of financial literacy, including the difference between assets and liabilities, and how to make your money work for you.

2. *I Will Teach You to Be Rich* by Ramit Sethi (IWillTeach YouToBeRich.com) offers a practical six-week personal finance program for twenty- and thirty-somethings.

3. *The Money Book for the Young, Fabulous & Broke* by Suze Orman provides investing and money management tips to help you solve your financial problems.

4. *Your Money: The Missing Manual* by J.D. Roth (GetRich Slowly.com) shows you how to eliminate debt, use credit properly, and manage expenses.

5. *10,001 Ways to Live Large on a Small Budget* by the writers of **WiseBread.com** teaches you how to live like a king, while spending like a peasant.

Smart entrepreneurs use logic and strategy to make purchasing decisions; they don't rely on ego and vanity. Successful entrepreneurs do what they have to do to sustain their life burn rates (more about this in Chapter 4). If that means eating Top Ramen instead of steak—or living with multiple roommates—then so be it. The key is to adapt your lifestyle to suit your business needs, and prioritizing your long-term goals over short-term luxuries.

Be smart about your finances. Deflate your ego before it deflates your wallet. Stop spending money frivolously and thinking you need to flash some style. Burn down the imaginary money tree that you grew in your head. It's not growing anything worthwhile, anyway.

3

DARWIN + MURPHY = REALITY

My first start-up was nothing short of a disaster.

In fact, it's now known among friends and colleagues as *the company that shalt not be named*. What started as a small, scalable, and simple service business quickly became a complex mess. Between rookie mistakes and unforeseen obstacles, my first company forever changed my perspective on business, and set me on a course to be a smarter, well-rounded entrepreneur.

The year was 2005. I had just graduated from NYU and formed a small entertainment production company. As I produced more and more projects I began to notice a trend: Big brands weren't just producing 30-second commercials, they were also integrating those commercials into multimedia campaigns that included Web sites, radio spots, Internet ads, and viral videos.

I remember thinking that it would be a great idea to get in on the action and add multimedia services to my company. I was already referring my clients to other service providers; I would just do it myself instead.

So I teamed up with a few media production pals to launch a one-stop-shop multimedia agency. It seemed like a logical progression for my entertainment production company to morph into a media production business. I would produce the video projects and my partners would manage the online media and audio projects. I'd now be able to sell my current clients on new media opportunities as well as benefit from my partners' existing client rosters.

It seemed like a no-brainer to me.

Had I known then what I know now, I'd have stopped myself from transforming my perfectly simple and profitable company into an overcomplicated money pit. But the sexiness of owning a media firm put twinkles in my eyes and blinded me from seeing the real problems that would lead to the company's eventual unraveling.

The day before our launch, my partners toasted to what a home run our start-up would be. After all, who wouldn't want low-cost media services?

Well, as it turned out, almost no one.

To put it mildly, *the company that shalt not be named* was far from a dream come true. On the good days it was a full-out nightmare that woke me up with cold sweats and the desire to find high ledges. On the bad days, I felt like I was strapped into the cockpit of a flaming jet plane taking a nosedive toward a mountain. The company folded in a little more than a year; it's unbelievable how many things went wrong in such a short amount of time:

- No one could pronounce the company's name properly.
- No one could read the contact information on our poor-quality, expensive business cards—and we couldn't afford new ones.
- Our failure to seek out new clients led to terrible sales cycles.
- I lost existing clients because they thought the new company lacked focus and core competency.
- We hired and fired a four-person workforce in a matter of two weeks because we couldn't afford them.
- Our first big client never paid us in full and actually left us in debt.
- Advisors threatened us with legal actions forcing us to incur a legal bill that was higher than our combined salaries.
- We invested six figures' worth of free services into a start-up in exchange for equity that never materialized.

- We lost a client project to a bigger competitor who then turned around and sub-contracted us to do the same work for less money than our original bid.
- We negotiated for months with a potential fourth partner who made big promises and never delivered.
- We nearly went broke pitching for investment money we didn't need.
- We acted on advice that nearly crippled the company on multiple occasions.
- Our best advisor died of a heart attack the day before he was going to begin introducing us to all of his clients and investor contacts.

Although my partners and I had the best intentions, we were far from innocent sheep when it came to running *the company that shalt not be named*. However, the major reason we also crashed and burned was because we became victims of our own belief in several start-up myths, entrepreneurial misconceptions, and business falsehoods.

I hope you're fortunate enough not to experience the same level of failure that I experienced with my first venture. However, you can benefit from my experience by avoiding these pitfalls on your entrepreneurial journey.

YOUR BUSINESS IS NOT THE EXCEPTION TO ANY RULE

I know how excited you are about your business idea. You can't wait to move mountains and become a captain of industry. I have no doubt you truly believe that your concept is a *guaranteed* winner. However, in reality, your idea is but a small part of the success equation. Besides, most people think they have a winner and the odds apply to you just as much as the next guy. According to the U.S. Small Business Association one-third of small businesses fail by their second year and less than half make it to four years.

Giving status quo the finger isn't easy and launching a business isn't a cakewalk. It's great to be passionate about your idea, but get it out of your head that your business is an exception to any rule.

It's not going to be easy. Deal with it. Don't become an entrepreneur if you're looking for an easy way to make a living. Running a start-up will push you to the limits; it's not glamorous and can stress out the calmest of individuals. You may even find yourself wanting to quit three or four times in the first two months and hundreds of times during the first six months—if you make it that long.

It is much harder to be your own boss than to have one. You can't expect a check to magically appear in your mailbox simply because you pasted a number on your vision board. Sure, if you're employed or have ever been employed, your boss might not know that he's paying you 10 hours each week to watch cat videos on YouTube and update your Facebook status, but in a start-up every moment you waste is a moment closer to bankruptcy.

You're going to fail often. Accept it. For the first time in your life, you will have to truly work your ass off to earn every dollar in your pocket and you will have to work harder than you've ever worked before. In the earliest stages of your business, you'll have to downgrade your lifestyle to absolute bare necessities and make your business your priority—milking it for every dollar of revenue it can provide.

Contrary to popular belief, failure is not such a bad thing. Hard-learned lessons from failures will guide you to successes, where you will reap the financial rewards for your own work. Your life might get harder before it gets easier, but if you want to win big at the risk-reward game now is the time to put the mission before the man—when you're young, hungry, and contain insurmountable amounts of energy.

Take your perfect plan and shove it. The right hypothetical team plus hip Google AdWords plus a funky sales presentation may sound like a winning combination on paper, but in reality, you know what it will most likely amount to?

Nada.

There is no magic start-up formula for you in a "Six Minute Start-Up" DVD. And the road less traveled is likely to lead you straight off a cliff.

Any successful entrepreneur will tell you that you can't predict future sales, revenues, and market acceptance for a start-up. It's simply impossible. Anyone who tells you otherwise doesn't know his or her ass from an elbow. Other than what you do and how you do it, you don't know as much as you think you know about your business or industry. Any idiot can write a business plan that paints a rosy picture about a hypothetical company. Truth be told, there is no such thing as the perfect plan.

Your product or service won't gain attention in the cluttered marketplace just because you plan everything to the letter. Don't be sucked into fictitious numbers and creating a business plan any longer than a paragraph (see Chapter 5). Besides, the best business plans are fluid, not set in stone.

Your product will not sell itself. Remember the riddle about the tree falling in the woods when no one is there to hear it? Does the tree make a sound? The business equivalent is launching a Web site and no one knows the URL. Does the Web site really exist? The answer is no. Buzz and customers will not materialize out of thin air. If you go into your start-up thinking that you'll be on easy street, the only street you'll be on is the one outside of your parents' house.

Great ideas don't launch and sell out instantly. There are millions of stimuli vying for a consumer's attention every second of every day and there are many factors that contribute to the success of hot-ticket, must-have products and services. You'll have to keep up with unpredictable trends, deal with consumer income fluctuating with the economy, effectively respond to market demand rising and falling without warning, and other such challenges that will always seem to hit you at the most inopportune times. This is why planning for your rock-bottom, worst-case scenario is absolutely essential and will help you to understand what might not—and often will not—go according to plan (more on planning for rock bottom later in this chapter).

First doesn't always mean number one. Being the first to market a particular product or service isn't always an advantage. Sometimes being first can actually put you in last place. The execution of your ideas will be the key to your company's success, not arbitrarily shooting to be the first in the market.

The competition is tough. If you find yourself with an idea you truly believe has no competitors, you are assessing your market with tunnel vision.

Every viable business has competition. If you delude yourself into thinking that there are no competitors in your target market, you should save your incorporation fees because declaring bankruptcy will cost you more money in legal fees later. Just because your start-up combines a dog-walking service with a lingerie store, doesn't mean you won't face competition from individual dog-walking services and lingerie stores. A small town bar is still in competition with restaurants and other nightlife activities. A Web site that sells flower arrangements will still compete with brick-and-mortar flower retailers.

Reality check: You are not alone and competitors will point out the error of your ways as loudly as possible to any potential customers who will listen.

Competitors will try to strike at you from every direction at every opportunity. Like you, they'll find ways to adapt to shifts in the market and use your own tactics against you. Big companies will try to swallow you, while smaller companies will nibble at your bottom line by undercutting your already low prices. If you come out with a great cost-effective product, a competitor will knock you off and lower the price point.

Business is about survival of the fittest, so if you want to stay in the game, you have to stay fit and on your toes.

Entrepreneurs are not high-risk gamblers out for a fast payday. TV has warped your perception of entrepreneurs as thrill seekers with a go-big-or-go-home mentality. Entrepreneurs take calculated risks while working to build steady and effective growth. Smart business owners weigh the pros and cons of every decision, spend money with extreme caution, manage the growth of their companies methodically, and play it as safe as possible.

Real entrepreneurs see betting the farm as a suicide mission, not a gamble.

Pushing for overexpansion, multiple services or product lines, or excessive growth will cripple you if you don't have the infrastructure to meet the demand or if it means that the quality of your product or service has to suffer.

Be cautious and set a reasonable risk threshold. Entertain as many options, potential solutions, and opportunities as possible before coming to a final decision on any matter. However, make sure to perform these exercises in a timely fashion so as not to hinder your revenue-generating momentum. Create a scalability plan for growing your business with demand and the necessary expansion-supporting revenue—not just in the name of the big risk.

Check your preconceived notions at the door. Building a business in theory and actually building a business are entirely different. Common sense will play a huge role during your start-up journey. For example, theoretically you might hand a prospective client a business card, she'd put the card in her Rolodex, and give you a call when she needs your service. Right?

If only it were so easy.

Reality might play out a little more like this: The prospective customer you met at an open-bar function probably forgot your name shortly after meeting you. She probably took your card and either never looked at it or lost it. To build a successful business, you need to understand the difference between the *theoretical* and the *actual* in order to plan for reality. Just because Facebook has hundreds of millions of users doesn't mean that you'll attract even a fraction of a percent of them to your Fan Page. Similarly, just because your niche market has thousands of potential prospects, doesn't mean that you're guaranteed to sell even one.

The only safe assumption is that growing a business made out of hopes and dreams will leave you vulnerable to collapse at the first storm.

Flawed common sense will inhibit your perceptions of reality. Avoid being an eternal optimist. Be a cautious pessimist and your business will be better off as a result.

Don't be General Custer. General Custer was *not* a great leader, otherwise he wouldn't have blindly led his legions to certain doom.

There is a huge difference between broken and unfixable.

If your market has vanished, your cash flow is nonexistent or you're taking substantial personal and financial risk without any light at the end of the tunnel, you're likely on a fool's errand for the sake of ego.

Decide your walk-away point *before* you launch your company, not when you're facing bankruptcy. Knowing your threshold at the gate will keep you from jumping off the deep end. If your idea doesn't pan out, reflect on what went wrong, what worked, and what mistakes you made. Assess what could have been done differently. Determine how you will utilize these hard-learned lessons to better yourself and your future entrepreneurial endeavors. Take it from me: A true entrepreneur finds ways to prevail over adversity and turns failures into life lessons—and turns life lessons into revenue.

THE WORST-CASE SCENARIO IS THE ONLY SCENARIO

Nothing will go as planned. Ever.

Plans change, businesses change, and markets change. Your world will be flipped upside down on a daily basis. Even the best-laid plans and the best intentions will find a way to go belly up. Failures are inevitable.

Your phone won't ring. You'll receive creditor statements more often than accounts receivable checks. Marketing objectives won't meet expectations. You'll spend a fortune on something totally ineffective. You'll predict $10,000 in revenue for the first quarter and be lucky to earn $250. Forget thousands of people coming to your Web site; you'll be lucky to attract 10 unique visits per day.

You get the idea.

Not only are you going to be wrong, but you're going to be wrong often. And that's okay. You need to learn to fail like a pro, adapt, and pay attention to details so you can make informed decisions that keep your business moving forward. How you preplan for failure and maneuver around unforeseen circumstances and harsh realities will be the key to finding success as your own boss.

The best way to avoid failure is to dissect every potential decision and to determine its worst possible outcome— or subsequent worst-case scenarios—that will stem from it being realized. I call this planning for your "rock bottom." The more you think about how you can avoid rock bottom, the more often you'll find yourself at the top. Some rock-bottom planning can be done prior to your launch, but unless you have ESP, rock-bottom planning is part of every decision you make.

As you learn to plan for the rock bottom in every situation, you'll become a smarter, more resilient entrepreneur. Your skills will improve as you begin to analyze success and failure more regularly. But remember to be honest with yourself. Sugar-coating this process or failing to learn from your mistakes will render your rock-bottom plan pointless and undoubtedly will get you into trouble. You should take the following four steps before making every business decision:

1. **Weigh the pros against the cons.** Do the pros of the best-case scenario wholly outweigh the cons of a potential rock bottom so much that the decision seems like a no-brainer? Or perhaps the pros and cons are so evenly matched that after careful consideration, the risks are simply far too great. In the case of the dead advisor I mentioned earlier, you might say: "How could I ever have planned for that in a million years." To which I would respond, I could have figured out how much stock I was putting into that one person and avoided putting all of my eggs into one basket.

2. **Determine the potential fallout if your decision's outcome goes south.** Will the rock bottom cripple the company's finances? How hard will it be to bounce back after a potential failure of this magnitude? Will your decision affect other decisions and company activities?

3. **Determine if this is an "at the time" decision or an "anytime" decision.** There's no doubt you've heard someone say that something seemed like a good idea "at the time." Avoid "at the time" regrets by thinking through the short-term, midterm, and long-term impacts of your decision. If you can imagine saying this phrase later, that should be a red flag warning.

4. **Consider alternatives to ensure your course of action is best.** If you couldn't execute your plan A, what would B, C, and D look like? Are B, C, and D better alternatives than A based on your rock-bottom planning? Or are B, C, and D better backup plans should A hit rock bottom? For example, is outsourcing or paying a monthly service fee

a better alternative to hiring a part-time Web developer for your start-up's Web site? This analysis will help you to determine if your original plan holds water or if a change in direction is warranted.

NO ONE WILL INVEST IN YOUR IDEA

Guess what. No one will invest in your idea. There, I said it. In fact, let me say that again because it bears repeating:

No one will invest in your idea!

I had considered bolding and underlining the sentence as well, but I assume you get the point.

No investors want you to lose their money. When you actively tell people that you need money to "make a business work," you are actually telling them that you don't have a business, you're clueless and lazy, your business is a long shot, and you want to take a gamble with their money.

Good luck with that.

In the eyes of investors, you're far from credible, reliable, or viable. Banks won't lend without proven management, years' worth of historical financial data, and substantial collateral. Angel investors see hundreds of thousands of businesses each year and the majority goes unfunded. Venture capitalists won't acknowledge your existence. Nor should they. If you haven't created or produced anything and you're already asking for money, but you still truly believe that you need millions to launch your start-up, you offer absolutely nothing of value to them and deserve absolutely no attention.

Forget about raising investment capital. At this stage in the game it's not a real option. Get it out of your head!

Entrepreneurship is a beginner's sport, not a banker's sport. Building a business is more about ingenuity and hustle than obtaining a wad of cash—which is why young people are the ideal candidates to build businesses. Compared to older

Six Fund-Raising Pillars to Attract Investors

Without a successful business under your belt, investment dollars won't be coming your way anytime soon. Don't even try to raise capital until your business has a handle on all six of these fundraising pillars. Otherwise, real investors and lenders won't even give you the time of day:

1. **History.** Inspire confidence with facts, not fiction. Companies built from the ground up have a huge advantage over those seeking start-up capital because they have proven they are *real* businesses with *real* customers and *real* revenues. Your company must have cash flow, a track record, and real-world experience before any credible investor will listen to what you have to say.

2. **Equity.** The only thing investors and lenders care about more than making money is getting their money back. And the only way to do that is to base their investments on something with real value that they can sell off if times get rough. Banks may ask for personal guarantees supported by a home and investors might tie their money to a company's patent. Either way, know that investors care about their money before your property.

3. **Leadership.** Money people invest in operations people, not businesses. Your leadership abilities must inspire investors. They have to believe that their investments are in capable hands and that you can effectively execute a strategy.

4. **Stewardship.** Your company must be debt-free, or close to it. Red balance sheets are nonstarters for most investors. No one wants to be responsible for paying off someone else's mistakes or debt.

(*continued*)

(*continued*)

5. **No Liability**. Your business must be clear of any pending or active litigations or lawsuits and free from personal or business debts that could endanger the company—or more importantly—the investor's money. If you can't pass a background or credit check, you won't be getting a check—period. But don't lie. Lies and partial truths will end up hurting your company and your relationships with investors in the future.

6. **Direction**. Get investors excited about the big picture, but be reasonable and responsible. Avoid hockey stick projections. Respectable investors will not take you seriously if you present them with nonsensical financial graphs that claim your company's revenues will grow from $100,000 to $50 million in three years—if *only* they would invest. Show investors that you have a grasp on reality by clearly outlining how you plan to use their funds.

Remember, getting outside financing still doesn't offer any guarantee of success—all it guarantees you is more mouths to feed before you can feed yourself and more cooks in your kitchen. It also means trading in many of the freedoms you worked so hard to achieve—and could even mean giving up the controlling stake in your business.

If you take on any investor—and that's a big if—be sure to do your due diligence. Don't just take money for the sake of taking money. Know what else your investors have invested in, what they specialize in, their track records, how deep their pockets are and what they bring to the table besides cash. Make decisions based on what's best for your business, not the investor.

generations, we have minimal living expenses and have the ability to scale down our lifestyles dramatically without major consequences. We also have the ability to bounce back after rock bottom far easier. And our belief that we can do anything drives us to solve problems.

The best businesses are built with blood, sweat, and tears, not funding. Your personal energies are far more important and valuable than any investment dollars anyway. This is why it is important not to overlook your most valuable asset: time.

Use time wisely and effectively. There is never enough of it and there never will be enough of it. Money comes and goes, but when your time is gone, it's gone forever. The beauty of entrepreneurship is being able to put every hour into something that benefits you directly. You are actively investing in your future with every decision and every sale.

Now it's time to teach you to do just that—invest in yourself and generate income as a result.

PART II

BUILDING A FOUNDATION

PART I

4

Get Off
Your Ass and
Start Up!

The closest thing I've ever had to a "real" job was an internship at an independent film production company during college.

I was fired in a little more than a month.

It was my second semester of sophomore year at NYU. I found myself spending many a Friday and Saturday night staying in, fleshing out a small business concept that I planned to launch on campus to earn a few extra bucks. A week or so before I was about to get going, I received an e-mail from my career advisor reminding me to attend a previously scheduled appointment the following day. I'd forgotten about the meeting entirely, and in hindsight, I wish I hadn't been reminded.

During our meeting the next day, my career counselor droned on about how important internships are and strongly encouraged me to look into securing one. Although internships weren't mandatory, he thought it would be a great opportunity for me to "experience" my industry and gain "invaluable" knowledge.

So my own business venture took a backseat while I searched the career center's database and scheduled an interview with what seemed like a reputable company. I was hired on the spot, congratulated by my future boss, and asked to start immediately. I found out later that congratulations were hardly in order. Every candidate was accepted, regardless of qualifications.

My college workload, social commitments, and three-day-a-week internship became nearly unmanageable. I quickly realized that my entrepreneurial ambitions were going to have to be put on hold indefinitely. I shelved my start-up again, and told myself it was just until I found more free time.

Two weeks passed—and the internship got worse by the day. Valuable experience, my ass. I wasn't learning a damn thing about the entertainment business. Each day my fellow indentured servants and I were reduced to file clerks and office gophers who fetched coffee and lunch for our superiors. Only if we were lucky did we receive the occasional chance to read and critique scripts as the internship description had indicated.

However—the worst part of the gig *by far* was the power-drunk middle manager whose severe anger issues earned him the nickname "Director Dickhead."

A month or so into the internship I was invited to have lunch with some of the top-level executives. When they asked about my experience working at the company, I smiled like an idiot, and lied my ass off. When they inquired about my opinion on the company's script review and evaluation process, I answered with what I believed were innocent suggestions to help the company organize, categorize, and evaluate the scripts more carefully and thoroughly.

I thought that was the end of it. But as it turns out, I was *very* wrong.

Word about my brief conversation got back to Director Dickhead, who—wouldn't you know it—was actually the creator of the archaic system on which I was asked to comment. Out of nowhere, he reminded me that I was just a lowly intern and that I was to keep my mouth shut. Suffice it to say it wasn't long before I was unceremoniously let go.

I was dejected and bitter and—to top it all off—I found out that another student had recently launched a start-up with an almost identical concept as the one I had been putting on hold. Not only was I now without an internship, but my start-up idea seemed to be dead in the water. I felt like I had lost out because I did what someone else expected of me instead of following my own instincts and exploring my own interests.

It was at that moment that I decided to never again allow myself to fall into the trap of becoming distracted from my entrepreneurial ambitions.

Now is the time for you to do the same and get rid of that miserable bastard known as the "real" job. No longer should you slog it out for the benefit of others, or let shareholders, idiot bosses, and dismal job markets decide how you make your living. It's time for you to delete or set fire to your resumes or tell your employers where they can shove that imaginary gold watch and stick that useless employee of the month certificate.

However—before you can open the doors to your new dream job and overcome your paycheck dependency syndrome, your business idea must first survive a series of tests designed to make sure that it has what it takes to make it in the real world.

GET REAL WITH YOUR FINANCES

Fact: Without you, there isn't a business. You and your start-up are one in the same. You share the same wallet, breathe the same air, and thrive (or nose dive) based on the same experiences, but you aren't in sync quite yet, or even on the same page. Before you can put pen to paper to flesh out your big idea, you must fully understand, deconstruct, and modify your financial life—so that you'll be prepared to make smart fiscal decisions based on fact.

How much is your life worth? Mind you, I'm not asking you to pull a nonsensical, hypothetical figure out of thin air in an attempt to make you feel better about yourself. Instead, you need to calculate a tangible number that corresponds to liquid capital—or assets that could be liquidated—that you currently possess.

Unless you've suddenly inherited property or forgot about your flourishing stock portfolio, the cash in your checking and savings accounts—and possibly a few inheritances from good old granny—will make up the majority of your assets. Amassing your bankroll will help you to determine your available start-up funds as well as the length of time in which you can sustain yourself without making a single penny. Obviously, if you don't have a dime to your name, this exercise should be relatively simple.

Prince or pauper? Many consultants and so-called experts spout oversimplified sound bites about cutting all your expenses in half. This is utterly useless advice. Only a small part of the equation is cutting down on expenses. You need to do something far more dramatic: Reprogram the way you think about money.

A real wake-up call can be developing a clear picture of your financial situation. Every dollar counts, and the little expenses you tend to overlook often add up to jaw-dropping totals. The first time that I sat down and analyzed my annual expenditures, I found that I had spent nearly $500 on ATM fees and $1,500 on NYC taxis—unreal! Regularly reviewing your finances can help you locate money you didn't know you had and decide judiciously what expenses can stay, what needs to be reduced, and what should be eliminated altogether.

What's your life burn rate? There's no denying it: You need a certain amount of monthly income to survive and sustain yourself. I call this your life burn rate. Definitively knowing—and subsequently editing and revising—your life burn rate is essential to determining the types of companies you'll be able to start.

Examine your expenditures from the previous year. How much money did you spend each month, and on what? Break down your expenses into three categories:

1. **Essentials:** Things you need to survive such as food, clothing, and shelter.

2. **Liabilities:** Recurring expenses you have no choice but to pay, such as student loans.

3. **Expendables:** One-time luxuries such as entertainment or taxi rides.

Then find a way to make cuts in each category.

Essentials. Where could you have used your money more efficiently? What inconsequential substitutions could you have made to save a little here and a little there? What purchases could you have avoided entirely? With each substitution, increase the severity of the cut to give yourself a wide range of savings options. For example, if you are thinking about ways to save money on rent, the option with the least amount of savings and lowest impact to your lifestyle might be to live with a roommate—whereas the option with the highest amount of savings and largest impact to your lifestyle is to move back in with your parents. In the end, you're the one who needs to weigh the cost-benefit analysis for each category that works best for you.

Liabilities. How much of your money was spent on liabilities? Much like the approach you took with the essentials category, determine three potential alternatives for each liability. Paid a lot of money in taxes? Maybe you or your accountant can find new write-offs you didn't previously consider. High credit card debt? Maybe you can consolidate all of the debt onto a single zero-or-low-interest card. College loans killing you? Perhaps you can renegotiate your monthly payments by refinancing with a different bank.

Expendables. This is often the biggest eye opener—because no matter what the number is, it will always seem absurdly high. What luxuries can you limit or reduce? Which can you eliminate entirely? For some, it might be as simple as eating out fewer times per month. For others, it might be a major overhaul such as getting rid of a car in favor of public transportation, cutting down on travel, and putting a strict cap on recreational activities. I'm not advocating that you live like an impoverished monk in a cave—but you can't have it all. If you plan to keep any of your luxuries, you need to choose them wisely. Learn to see these more extravagant items as goal purchases rather than impulse buys. Make them rewards; this will motivate you to work that much harder and save you a boatload of cash in the interim.

Use the following formula to calculate your life burn rate:

$$\left.\begin{array}{l}\text{Revised Monthly Essentials} + \\ \text{Revised Monthly Liabilities} + \\ \text{Revised Monthly Expendables}\end{array}\right\} = \text{Your Monthly Life Burn Rate}$$

Once you've calculated your life burn rate, you can determine how long you can survive without making a single penny with the formula below:

$$\frac{\text{Liquid Capital}}{\text{Monthly Life Burn Rate}} = \text{Total Months You Can Stay Afloat Without Income}$$

Whether your total is zero or 15, use this information when brainstorming your business idea. All you'll have to get your business started is what you currently have; you can't count on outside funding. More importantly, your start-up will need to—at a minimum—allow you to break even based on your life burn rate.

The test of your new fiscal responsibility comes in daily practice. Can you survive a day without straying from your new life burn rate? A week? A month? You'll undoubtedly find that some cuts work, and others don't. New experiences may prompt new ideas, alternatives, and cost-cutting techniques. Assess your method's effectiveness daily and adapt it as necessary. Don't treat this like some short-lived diet. This is a life-altering game plan and the first major step in your becoming your own boss.

Eight Tools to Cut Your Bills, Save You Money, and Keep Your Finances on Track

Cut costs, find bargains, and lower your life burn rate with these eight personal finance tools:

1. **Mint.com** is a free personal finance management tool that keeps track of your bank accounts, credit card bills, budgets, and financial transactions. Mint also compares and recommends financial products, such as credit cards and bank accounts, to ensure that you get the best prices. Cost: Free.
2. **BillShrink.com** enables you to slash expenses by helping you find the lowest price on essential expenses such as gas providers and wireless carriers. Cost: Free.
3. **Wesabe.com** is like an online team of financial advisors. This service combines practical budgeting tools to aggregate your financial life into one place with an online community that offers free advice to help you reach your personal saving and budgeting milestones. Cost: Free.
4. **NerdWallet.com** compares credit card rates and rewards to find the perfect card to fit your personal or business needs. Cost: Free.
5. **Coupons.com** is exactly what the URL implies: A repository for hundreds of thousands of offers with new coupons added every day. Cost: Free.
6. **PriceGrabber.com** lets you compare prices on millions of products to guarantee that when you buy almost anything it's at the lowest price possible. Cost: Free.
7. **Experian.com** provides you with a free annual credit score. Be sure to get this report every year to know exactly what your financial picture looks like. Cost: Free once per year.
8. **WiseBread.com** is a daily blog dedicated to helping readers make smart financial decisions and get the most out of their personal lives and businesses on small budgets. Cost: Free.

THOSE WHO REINVENT THE WHEEL ARE DOOMED TO BE RUN OVER BY IT

Your idea is not original—not by a long shot. There's a strong chance that someone with more funding, enhanced experience, and better contacts is doing the same thing as you right now. There's also a strong probability that similar business ideas have gone down in flames before.

Don't try to be original. You're not that smart—and really, you don't even need to be.

Originality will not skyrocket your bottom line or help you make a sale faster. In fact, quite the opposite—pushing products or services as "wholly original" or "totally unique" will force you into an unwinnable uphill battle. So-called original products unnecessarily complicate a simple business for the sake of making it appear more unique or sexy. This can lead to overblown pitches and a lack of consumer understanding or adoption. Just because you think something is a stroke of brilliance doesn't mean it's never been done before. I assure you that the world will be just fine without your solar powered flashlight, glass hammer, or waterproof towel.

*Un*original, on the other hand, works. Unoriginal is profitable.

You don't have to disrupt an entire industry to be successful. The vast majority of successful businesses produce products and services that are cheaper, faster, or better than some other guy. There is a reason that Hollywood continues to crank out crappy teen romance movies off the unoriginal assembly line. The proven formulas work (Any Bare-chested Male Model + Hillary Duff Look-alike + Vampires + Tweens = Cha Ching!).

Starting a sexy new business with an "original" revenue model is foolish and unproductive. Instead, use your branding and marketing strategies to distinguish your business from the competition. For example, a company called College Hunks Hauling Junk turned junk removal services into a unique, entertaining experience by having college jocks clean out homes. Starbucks turned the coffee shop into an assembly line with its own lingo.

Most successful businesses are based on ideas that have been executed before, or the derivatives of previously successful models. Learn from other businesses and adapt portions of their proven models to help you achieve sustainable success.

Seven Steps to Get Up and Running

Here are seven steps to turn your idea into a legal business.

1. **Amass a team of advisors.** The most important advisors are arguably your lawyer and an accountant. Find someone in your network of family or friends who is willing to accept a free lunch in exchange for letting you pick his or her brain about what you'll need to know about starting a business and handling its finances. Make sure that you do your homework to verify this person's qualifications. As your business grows, your advisors will be your first line of defense and will become indispensable members of your inner circle. Be careful not to take advantage of their time, but do ask all of the questions you need answered. Make it clear to them that they are investing in your growth, and you'll be happy to hire them once your start-up begins generating revenue.

2. **Choose a structure.** Consult with your lawyer and accountant about the most advantageous way to structure your business to protect it from liability, as well as the best approach for tax purposes. Ask them to lay out the pros and cons of each option based on the type of business you plan to start, how you plan to generate and receive income, and the city and state where you plan to incorporate.

3. **Research permits or licenses.** Research your town, city, and state's government Web sites to see if you will need any

permits to operate your business. Some permits are free or relatively inexpensive, but others can cost a fortune. Know what you are getting into before you throw away money on incorporation.

4. **Name your company.** Your company name will serve a vital role in your sales and marketing efforts. Later in the book, I offer you a few strategies about how to go about naming your company.

5. **Incorporate with LegalZoom.com.** This service is by far the most inexpensive and the easiest way to incorporate your business. However, keep in mind that you do *not* need to incorporate right away. If you lack the funds to do so, test out your idea as a freelancer and have customers pay you directly until you have the necessary funds to form a legal entity. The only thing to remember is that you won't be able to open a business bank account or receive payments made out to your company name until you have been issued an EIN number by the government.

6. **Open a bank account in a local bank.** I always suggest working with local banks rather than regional or conglomerate ones. Local banks are much more willing to invest time into building personal, long-term relationships with community business owners. Once you prove that you can generate revenue, being on a first-name basis with local bank representatives might help you secure credit lines and loans more easily.

7. **Use DocStoc.com for agreement templates.** Before you even consider hiring a lawyer to draft any agreement from scratch, visit the document-sharing service DocStoc.com to see if free or inexpensive templates exist. This allows you to save a fortune by eliminating legal drafting fees and only having lawyers examine final drafts for approval.

WHAT DO YOU KNOW, ANYWAY?

There are many factors about which you're unaware when you start a business. However, there are also several things you know for absolute certain—things that will help you to plan a solid starting point for your business.

Know who you are. What do bleach companies with "green" product lines, fast-food companies promoting healthy exercise, and politicians kissing babies all have in common?

They're all bad liars who insult your intelligence by masquerading as something they're not.

Misleading business pitches and phony gestures are not going to fool anybody. Authenticity is vital to your success. The only result of trying to be something you're not is attaining a reputation as a snake oil salesperson or con artist. It can also wreak havoc on your start-up by causing you to lose consumer confidence faster than you can give a wink, click your tongue, point your imaginary hand gun, and sleazily say, "Trust me."

Don't try to be everything to everyone, or you'll end up being nothing to anyone. If you're a *Star Trek*–obsessed tech geek, wear Vulcan ears to meet your computer repair appointments. If you're a beach bum numbers guy, wear shades and flip-flops to your bookkeeping gigs.

Be true to yourself and own who you are. Customers need to trust, like, respect, and relate to you. You're already launching a start-up with little to no credibility, so avoid adding kindle to the fire by giving people a reason to question your integrity.

Know what you have. Manufacturing plants, delivery trucks, or acres of available land. You've got none of it. And although you might have a whole lot of nothing, at the same time you do have a little bit of *something*.

So what do you have?

When you brainstorm about what your starting point will be, you're better off only taking into account what you own or have access to through your network *before* making any purchases. What resources, tools, and services do you and your immediate friends, family, and contacts have at your fingertips? Can you use your mom's car for deliveries? Does one of your friends own a Crock-Pot and a set of good knives for cooking your specialty?

You'll be surprised to find that you have access to quite a few resources; you just have to do a bit of legwork. Steer clear of business ideas that require resources that aren't in your back pocket; this will undoubtedly hamper your ability to get your start-up off the ground. Be thorough in your analysis and don't overlook anything. You never know how important something is until you suddenly don't have it.

Know what you do. Do what you know. Know that you can do it. I always enjoy reading fiction—also known as 90 percent of all start-up how-to books and articles. The dreamscapes they paint always seem to have a knack for happy endings and glamorized brainstorming techniques.

Let your talents be your guide.
Transform your passions into profits.
Turn your hobbies into a business.
Do what makes you happy.

This is lovey-dovey utopian nonsense. Of course, you should never do something that you don't love to do. Duh. Thanks Sherlock. Disagreeing with these statements is the equivalent of saying that the sky is red or it's 95 degrees in Antarctica year-round.

Passions are vitally important, but passions won't pay your bills or enable you to make a living. Although it's important to love what you do—because you may well be doing it for the rest of your life—you still need to be able to turn these passions into companies that are capable of generating immediate revenue. These treatise-writing academics often fail to mention any of the following four key points that need to be considered when developing your business concept:

1. **Not all hobbies are meant to become the backbone of your entrepreneurial efforts**. Some hobbies are just that—hobbies. Knowing how to knit doesn't automatically mean it's a great idea to open a yarn shop. Hobbies can't just become businesses because they are fun or put a smile on your face; they must be easily transformed into a valuable and profitable simple service or product. Don't allow yourself to fabricate a fantasy world around becoming a professional LEGO builder.

2. **Even if you love something, you have to actually be able to *do* what you love**. And not just decently or okay either. You have to have expertise and be able to execute with absolute precision. Great, you enjoy skiing. If you suck at the sport, starting a ski school to train aspiring athletes for black diamonds probably isn't the best idea. Before you attempt to turn a hobby into a profitable enterprise, be honest with yourself about what your actual talents are—not what you think they are or what you'd like them to be.

3. **Just because *you* love your hobbies and passions, doesn't mean others will, too**. You need to make sure that your passion-turned-business provides something of value to others. Just because you want to sell it, doesn't mean anyone will buy it. Will your product help someone solve a problem? Does your service improve upon an existing service? Can it really help anyone do anything? Be realistic and down-to-earth in your assessment. If no one loves what you love, it's time to find something that people actually care about.

4. **Even if you love what you do and can do what you love, you need to make sure you *can* do it yourself—at least at the outset**. You won't be able to hire an in-house team

to execute; you need to be a one-person marching band on steroids. If you can't produce the product or provide the service with your own two hands, how do you plan to get started? You might love fixing cars or building custom furniture, but if your business can't get off the ground with you—and *only* you—don't even think you'll be avoiding a "real" job anytime soon.

Know what you want. No, you're not a fortune-teller. You can't see what's coming a month from now, let alone 10 years—and you shouldn't try. But it's important with any venture that you consider your long-term objectives from the beginning, and develop a plan with those goals in mind. Are you building a company to pass down to your children, or one that you plan to sell to the highest bidder as quickly as possible? Do you want to build the business on your own back, or eventually attract outside capital from angel investors or venture capitalists? Though these objectives will change, it's always a smart idea to set goals to keep you on track, play a strong role in your decision making, and motivate you to achieve milestones.

Whatever your goals may be, don't forget to keep your feet on the ground. Remember, irrational goals will lead to irrational decisions. Never let yourself say something as dumb as, "I'm starting a business to become a millionaire."

KEEP IT SIMPLE, STUPID

If you were learning to juggle, you'd start with two balls in one hand until you master the technique and train your hand-eye coordination. After a few weeks of practice, the fundamentals would slowly get easier. Eventually, you could be ready to add your second hand and two new balls into the mix. With the time and dedication, you could learn to master a three- or

four-ball routine. Perhaps one day you'd even be able to introduce bowling pins or flaming torches.

You should build your start-up the same way. But if you're
like most Gen Y entrepreneurs, you naively believe that you're
capable of juggling 2 flaming torches, 3 bowling pins, and 10
balls on day one without a single lesson. You might be thinking
that starting with one ball is too easy, too simple, or too small.
Well, guess what? This irrational logic is precisely the reason
you'll fail early, quit too soon, or go broke.

To build a business from the ground up, you must break
your concept down into its simplest form so you can manage
the processes yourself in the early stages. Though this exercise
may sound deceptively simple, it should not be taken lightly.
You may believe that your idea is as simplified as it can get—
but I assure you, you're totally off base.

Let's say that you want to open a gourmet burger restaurant using a cool "Burger Boogie" brand and tasty secret
sauce as the cornerstones for success—but unfortunately, you
couldn't afford to launch. You *insist* that not a single expense
can be spared. You *need* the glossy menus and the full kitchen.
And the great location is absolutely *essential* to making the
concept work.

You're right. You can't afford a restaurant. However, that
doesn't mean you can't own the greatest local burger joint ever.
All you need to do is eliminate the restaurant and you're all set!

Seems to me that you haven't simplified the concept. In
fact, you haven't even considered exactly how complex it
really is. Had you simplified, you'd be thinking more about
how to sell Burger Boogie burgers featuring your original
sauce recipe.

Was the word "restaurant" included in that idea? No. And it
shouldn't have been in there in the first place.

Rent would be cost-prohibitive; retrofitting a space would
cost a fortune; and professional kitchen equipment is just a

fantasy. Does this mean that you can't follow your dream? Absolutely not. All you need is to figure out what you have to work with and start working with what you have.

Maybe your parents have a basement that you can use as the base for your operation. Perhaps you can start with a delivery-only late-night menu targeted at local college students. Rather than pour thousands of dollars into rent and equipment, you could take portable grills to tailgating events or retrofit one to the back of your "Burger Moped." Instead of having customers experience your brand at a brick-and-mortar location, you can take your brand to them by wearing a cheesy "Burger Boogie" costume. The point is that many, if not all, of these suggestions would help you prove your concept on a shoestring budget, avoid infrastructure expenses, and afford you the opportunity to earn a living building a grassroots brand.

Your dream of owning a restaurant doesn't have to be dead. But it surely isn't step one. Your ego may be telling you differently, but unless your ego is hiding a few hundred thousand dollars, it would be best to tell your ego to shut the hell up.

Bottom line: You need to start somewhere or you'll never start at all.

Even a powerhouse like Google started as a simple search engine. Had they tried to be a search engine provider with mobile phone services, Web browsers, and online applications from day one, we might be asking Jeeves for much more advice today. Simplify your idea to its core to find ways to remove as many obstacles from your path as possible. Concentrate on creating a simple, singular service that focuses on the needs of a narrowly defined customer base. Then, brainstorm as many plausible ways to sell X product or service to Y customers for Z profit before you decide on a course of action. Throw convention out the window to open a whole new world of options.

Don't get caught up in your big picture; rather, give attention to the place where it can actually begin. After all, if you start with the flaming torches and bowling balls, you might find yourself in the emergency room with a broken foot, a singed scalp—and a massive medical bill to boot.

THE BOTTOMLESS MONEY PIT

Moneymaker or money pit? That is the *only* question.

Before you plan for your retirement, you first need to determine if your idea is based on passions, profits, or both. Just having a "great idea" doesn't mean that it will translate into a viable business.

I know you're convinced that people will chomp at the bit when they catch wind of your new Web site, MyExpensive SiteIsGoingtoBankruptMe.com. You may have even tricked yourself into believing that your idea is so brilliant the money question will just figure itself out later.

Let's get something straight: The correct answer for how your company will make money is not, "we'll figure out how to generate revenue later." Without a revenue model, *you do not have a business*. More importantly, without a revenue model neither you nor your business can survive. So if your first start-up's financial success is based on being acquired for billions or licensing unproven intellectual property to lunchbox companies, the only checks you'll be collecting are welfare.

Successful entrepreneurs work to generate money today, not tomorrow.

Wake up and smell the roses. If you've never made a dime with this idea before, there's no way you can predict, entertain, or defend a business model based on guesstimates, assumptions, or potential future success. If you really want to quit or avoid a "real" job and still earn a living, your business needs to be able to generate money day one, not—maybe—year 10. It's vital that you determine how, when, and if your idea can put money in your pocket; be it tomorrow, next month, or at all.

Seven Reasons to Rethink Your Business Idea

Not all business ideas are created equal—or profitable. To get out of the 9-to-5, you must start a company that's capable of producing immediate revenue to support your life burn rate. There are certain types of businesses that will not generate enough revenue to allow you to ditch your "real" job; as a result, these must be avoided entirely. This doesn't mean that you can't eventually pursue one of these types of businesses in the future—but go back to the drawing board if any of these seven characteristics reminds you of your idea.

1. **Based on a hypothetical exit strategy.** Your business will never have the chance to get acquired or go public if you go broke before you can get it off the ground. The end game isn't possible without a solid short game—and the short game requires you to make a living so that you can keep your business moving forward. I can't say it enough: Your start-up must produce immediate revenue, not be based on hypothetical paydays that will probably never happen. Get into a business because it can make money, not because a similar company you heard about in a magazine was acquired for eight figures.

2. **Major traction needed.** Traction-based businesses are typically Web-based subscription sites or Web sites supported by advertisements that take a lot of time and energy for little, if any, payoff nowadays. Massive traction does not just happen because you've got a great URL and good content. In fact, it usually never happens. Most Web sites today need to attract tens of thousands of unique visitors and clicks-per-page just to make a few dollars. You don't have time to wait and see if your business can attract a following. You

(continued)

(*continued*)

need to be able to sell someone something and generate immediate income as a result.

3. **Based on small margins.** Low-profit margin companies that earn you two cents on the dollar won't support your life burn rate. You need to concentrate your efforts on building a business with initial profit margins of 30 to 80 percent of the gross proceeds. As you scale your business in the future, your profit margin may decrease. However, being able to do a lot of work yourself in the beginning and being more successful as a result will be the reason you're able to make more money with smaller margins in the first place.

4. **Based on licensing unproven intellectual property.** Get real: Disney will not be busting down your door to license an unproven, untested animated character for TV shows and lunch boxes. Licensing is not a start-up business, it's a complex one with big players with big dollars at stake, and rarely does it ever favor start-up entrepreneurs. Don't base your primary revenue stream on a one-in-a-million dream shot. Work hard to build a great brand with a successful, repeatable business model—and maybe you'll be able to consider licensing or franchising the proven concept later on down the road.

5. **Target market is too limited.** If your business has to target behemoth corporations or the super rich—or there are only five applicable clients in the whole world—then just stop right now. You can't expect your company to only hit home runs—because it won't. Nor can it start with a severely limited pool of potential prospects to sell into. Instead, you need to develop a well-balanced offering, capable of generating cash flow from a wide niche market-place that supports clients big and small.

6. **Cost-prohibitive start-ups.** If you need big money to get in the game or big inventory to set up shop, scale it down, and simplify it—or drop it and move on. If you don't have it, you won't get it—and as I've said several times already, you'll go broke trying.

7. **Businesses you know nothing about.** Being a start-up that competes against established companies in your market already puts you at a disadvantage. What makes you think you can start a new company blind and expect to kill it in sales? You already have a learning curve when it comes to starting and operating a business; don't overcomplicate matters further by not having a clue about the product or service you plan to provide.

Defer to business models that rely on business-to-business sales, service fees, or other such models where sales are not based on circumstances that are entirely out of your control. In the longer term, you can always experiment or expand your business model to include ancillary, secondary, and longer-term revenue sources—but without immediate revenue, you'll go broke before you even have the chance to get ranked by a search engine.

CAN YOUR SWOT TEAM DO CPR?

"Can your SWOT team do CPR?" is a mnemonic device I turn to whenever I need to evaluate the merits, viability, and growth potential of a start-up. This memory aid will help you to scrutinize each aspect of your simple service or product—from concept to execution to distribution—and determine whether your idea holds water. Both of these exercises will help you fully evaluate an idea before you decide to open for business.

The first component of the mnemonic device is the acronym SWOT—Strengths, Weaknesses, Opportunities, and Threats. Not to suddenly go all MBA on you, but conducting a SWOT analysis will help you to analyze internal and external factors that will either positively or negatively affect your business.

Strengths. Identify strengths to help you validate your idea's intrinsic competitive advantages, and forecast how it will stand up against competition. Does your niche offering allow you to be a big fish in a small pond? Will your family name carry significant weight in your community? Will your small size help you to deliver your service to customers faster and more efficiently than larger competitors? Does your company offer something proprietary that competitors can't offer? Can you defend your turf with exclusivity agreements with key distributors?

Weaknesses. Uncover weaknesses to expose inherent problems with your concept and help you decide whether the idea is amendable or a lost cause. Does your idea suffer from a lack of competitive differentiation? Will the life span of your product's usefulness run out? Is it overhead-heavy or inventory-intensive? Will the lack of a brand name hurt you? Are there a large number of gatekeepers, licenses, permits, or barriers to entry standing in your way? Can larger competitors stomp you like a bug by outspending you? Will competitors be able to easily undercut your price point without breaking a sweat? Do you lack access to key distributors or necessary resources?

Opportunities. Determine opportunities to help you assess outside factors that will benefit your business's bottom line. Is there unclaimed market share up for grabs within your locale or region? Is your business part of a growing, evergreen market sector? Is there a lot of unfulfilled consumer demand for your product or service with minimal or inadequate suppliers?

Can your product or service be distributed through new national and international channels?

Threats. Forecast threats to alert you to external circumstances that can cripple the company and knock the wind out of your sails. Is your market too crowded with well-entrenched, well-funded competitors? Can consumer demand turn cold on a dime? Is there a possibility for government intervention or increased taxation on your industry? Is your market susceptible to an invasion by an overabundance of new competitors?

Analyze each element of your idea thoroughly and honestly. Do the strengths and opportunities outweigh its weaknesses and threats? Can certain drawbacks be converted into advantages? Be sure not to put a positive spin on anything that is truly a red flag. Sugarcoating or overlooking any weakness or threat will come back to bite you in the ass tenfold.

Now it's time to determine if your idea can do CPR: Copy, Paste, and Repeat. Performing a CPR analysis of your idea will help you to figure out if your idea is scalable, expandable, and replicable.

Copy. Scalability and the ease of scalability are vital components to your business's long-term profitability and growth. Companies that can be stabilized and streamlined can be transformed into turnkey operations that are fully prepared for exponential growth. Will your overall costs drop as production and automation become more efficient? Will your business be capable of scaling up and down with ease based on supply and demand? Do you foresee a moment in your business's evolution where you will be able to create an ironclad formula for success—such as X Hard Costs $+$ Y Marketing $=$ Z Profit and replicate its tried-and-true results?

Paste. Businesses with strong expansion capabilities can capture more market share and seamlessly move into new markets without altering their existing model. Can your business model be applied to scores of new vertical markets? Is it able to quickly capitalize on new trends without significant modifications? In short—can you paste your model into any market or situation and make it profitable?

Repeat. Companies that can recreate optimal conditions and replicate previous successes are prime candidates for large-scale or exponential growth. Can new offshoots and subsidiaries be plug-and-play? Would a new business unit have the opportunity to reconstruct the successes enjoyed by the original? Will your new units be able to prosper if you remove yourself from the mix? Will it matter where your business is located in order to attract consumers and gain market share?

If your idea can stay alive after getting shot to hell by your SWOT team and survive surgery with CPR, then the chances that you have a real business with true potential are all the more likely.

5

BUSINESS PLANS SUCK

What was the only thing worse than the *company that shalt not be named* itself? That would be the process of writing its business plan.

As a hungry new entrepreneur who didn't know any better, I was worried about my business plan being done "exactly right" and "by the book." I now despise such phrases and consider them telltale signs of naïve and inexperienced entrepreneurs.

So many people and their mothers told my partners and me that we needed a "traditional business plan" to be successful. So we set out to do our business plan homework; reading lengthy books, studying sample plans, and filling out tedious worksheets and templates. We completed the first draft of our plan several weeks after we began: A 10-page document that outlined our media services and mission statement and summarized how we planned to sell X service to Y customer and make our hypothetical Z profit.

I wish it had ended there. Unfortunately, the conciseness of that first business plan didn't last long. Slowly but surely, we let the plan become a full-blown business in and of itself.

The nonsensical financial forecasts, complicated statistics, and intricate details about mundane marketing tactics were only the tip of the iceberg. Impromptu brainstorm sessions somehow morphed into five-page additions. Hours upon hours were wasted rewriting the body to make it "sound" better. Our sections went from short and simple to exhausting and overly complex. At the recommendation of every so-called business plan expert, we'd change the entire plan's formatting and structure.

We kept right on writing, foolishly believing that a more detailed document also added substance to our business model, and would force us to conceive of better sales and marketing strategies—and, as a result, offer us a greater likelihood of success. We also thought that a traditional business plan would ensure that we'd get the funding we needed.

Sadly, that's not what happened.

Ninety-four pages, 23 sections, and 19 weeks later, our traditional business plan for our simple little start-up had become a convoluted, unrecognizable mess. The sheer thickness of the document resembled a telephone book. But these weren't the only things wrong with this overpriced paperweight.

- Our plan was 70 percent focused on what we would *eventually* do, 20 percent focused on our industry and partner bios, and only 10 percent focused on what we could *currently* do.
- We focused too closely on the plan's grammar and formatting, and not enough on the actual business's sales and production efforts.
- From parents to advisors, we revised our plan based on *every single reader's* comments—without regard as to whether they were qualified to offer such advice.
- We spent weeks designing the plan to make it look "pretty"—a move that resulted in our spending $50 to $65 in ink, bindings, and supplies whenever we needed a copy.
- We failed to do real-world tests when trying a new marketing tactic before we revised the almighty plan.
- The financials were laughably inflated; they predicted unachievable revenues of $200 million by year three.

Suffice it to say, this archaic, inane, and time-consuming process did nothing more than cripple our productivity, divert our attention from our start-up, and bury us in minutia and busy work. Outside of the partners, our families, and paid advisors, only five other people ever read the final document—none of whom became clients or investors.

So nothing gets my blood boiling more nowadays than listening to dinosaurs who are 50 years my elder rant about the importance of a traditionally structured business plan. In a day and age where banks refuse to lend to start-ups and the Internet can render the printed word obsolete before it hits the printer, it boggles my mind that any sane individuals still tout this old-fashioned, rigid process as relevant or even useful. Traditional cookie-cutter business plans—as we know them today—are impractical exercises for start-ups. They do nothing but fuel procrastination and scare aspiring entrepreneurs into purchasing overpriced textbooks and software. Sure, it's indisputably true that business planning is essential for any start-up; however, the tools and materials you produce need not be remnant of the business world circa 1985.

It's time to strike a match and host a business plan book-burning party!

Business planning is not a revenue-generating activity. Rather, the actual money-making exists in the plan's execution. Therefore, it is imperative that business planning generates the action plan you need as quickly as possible—so you can start selling immediately. Unlike creating a passive, static traditional business plan that might as well get shoved in a dresser drawer, the tools you will produce will provide you with living, breathing, and fluid action plans that you can use daily. This methodology will keep you thinking on your feet and help you to plan your business strategy as you move your start-up forward.

TOSS THE OLD-SCHOOL BUSINESS PLAN

The first step to overcoming your business plan dependency is realizing that traditional business plans are not synonymous with success. Similarly to how your mentors failed you by selling you the whole "work hard, go to college, get a good job and a good life" dream, a parallel group is trying to convince you that writing your untested, unsubstantiated idea in a specific format will make your company a viable business and/or eligible for investment money.

You must rid yourself of the nonsense you've been spoon-fed by pundits, professors, and business plan "experts." Instead, focus your efforts on building a solid business, rather than writing the perfect plan.

Avoid business plan books and software like the plague. Publishers, software developers, and corporations generate millions of dollars peddling business-planning books, products, and programs to aspiring and amateur entrepreneurs. They also reinforce their business plan manifesto at every opportunity, because they need to suck us in and keep us addicted.

Let me save you a trip to the garbage can: Don't bother with any of these time and money wasters. What I'm about to tell you will be more practical to your start-up than any 250-page textbook: The only things you need to develop effective strategies are your brain, intuition, and common sense. Not only will those other remedial planning materials burn a hole in your wallet, they will overwhelm you with unnecessary work-sheets. If you really have an urge to fill in some blanks, go buy a MadLibs.

Never use traditional business plans for samples. The only thing more useless than reading a business plan book is reading someone else's business plan. What do you expect to learn from someone else's plan? Formatting tips? The proper way to structure a table of contents? What other people wrote about *their* businesses? I assure you that your dog-walking company will gain nothing from looking at plans for Mary Jo's Cleaners or Sam's Car Wash. More often than not, free plans are nothing more than sales tools disguised by business plan product companies to look like online resources. Most of the time, their only goals are to lure you into making a purchase.

The only time you should bother reading someone else's traditional business plan is if it outlines a business model similar to yours, and you can directly benefit from its *content*. Otherwise, don't concern yourself with how other people wrote their plans. All this exercise will do is sucker you into plagiarism—and trick you into writing a useless document.

Only the *right* people should ever read your work. Unless your parents, friends, teachers, or colleagues are partners in your venture or have the ability to offer valuable and relevant insight—that's based on real-world experiences—then don't bother asking them for opinions on your business-planning efforts.

It's not their business, after all: It's yours!

Validation, grammar corrections, and general feedback are not good enough reasons to bring someone inside your inner planning circle. Only let individuals who can truly add value assist you during your business-planning process. Keep your judgment unclouded and don't just give anyone and everyone the right to become a cook in your kitchen. Make sure that your planning mentors are qualified before inviting their interpretation. If you can't think of any direct questions for an individual then don't even bother to value or entertain that person's opinions.

Don't try to impress imaginary bankers, angel investors, and venture capitalists. Wake up: Who do you think will be reading your start-up's business plan? Banks won't. Investors won't. No one will believe that your business is more than just words printed on a page until the moment you demonstrate and prove its viability with *real* revenues and profits. To them, it's not about what you say you *will* do; it's about saying what you *did*, and the lucrative results of those efforts.

The biggest mistake you can make is planning a strategy with the wrong person's needs in mind. Never include anything in your planning tools simply because it sounds or looks good or contains information you think other people need to hear. I assure you that they won't be listening or caring about you or your business. Stop concerning yourself with them and worry about yourself, your product or service, and your target market. Your plan must be for you and *only* you. Simply produce a strategy based on what's doable, practical, and makes good sense for your company—one that will help you to turn your words into profitable realities.

Nothing is ever written in stone. The real world isn't simple, static, or stationary. This remains true whether your business goes bust or knocks one out of the park. Both a business and its environment can change on a dime. Don't be afraid to follow your gut instincts. Savvy entrepreneurs adapt as the environment changes. They don't rely on old information—old meaning anything older than the absolute present. Modifying your course is not always a bad idea; in fact, it's usually necessary to do so. Never let a plan hold you back or be the "final say" in your business's direction. You dictate the business, and the business dictates the plan—not the other way around.

This is no time to be an English teacher. Don't get caught up with remedial activities like spelling or grammar. Should your company go on to generate millions of dollars, investors won't turn you down because your business plan resembles a fifth grader's homework assignment with fragments and run-on sentences. Besides, you'll be paying someone else to write your plan by then, because you'll be too busy growing your business.

Use real-people language. All of the tools you produce must be quick reads and references. Write plainly and matter-of-factly. Avoid tech talk, business jargon, buzzwords, sales speak, and verbose, thesaurus-ridden prose. The only thing smart about "smart talk" is avoiding it entirely.

Save a tree; skip the fluff. Business planning isn't meant to be a creative-writing exercise. If something isn't important, don't include it. Get to the meat and potatoes. Each and every word needs to be useful, focused, and purposeful. Stay on point—you'll be better for it.

Skip the cutesy crap. Do you feel the need to surround yourself with colorful graphs and pretty charts? Then steal a kindergartener's artwork and put it on your refrigerator. No one's going to reward you with a gold star or extra credit for creativity. Don't waste time designing business-planning documents. They need to make money, not win a pageant.

Avoid factoids and data dumps. Being a successful entrepreneur is not about diagrams, stats, and charts. It's about getting off your ass, securing a meeting, and selling something to someone else to generate income. This isn't the time for writing a term paper—so don't concern yourself with statistics that claim your business is part of a $10 billion industry. No one else cares—and neither should you. After all, what percentage of that figure is in your bank account? Not much, I wager. Let your amateur competitors waste time writing dissertations backed to the hilt with mounds of facts and data. You've got market share to capture.

Don't play with Monopoly money. I'm truly glad that you plan to reinvest 30 percent of your profits into your marketing budget once you generate $10,000 in revenue. However, how do you intend to create that amount of income in the first place? Your business plan cannot write checks. If you have $0— well, then, you need to plan for $0. Only plan with the cash and resources you currently have in hand. Keep your life burn rate in mind every step of the way.

If you wouldn't do it, then they won't either. No matter how wonderful you think a marketing tactic may be or how perfect you think a service offering sounds, if *you* wouldn't buy into it, *they* won't either. Scrap it. Bad assumptions lead to poor business decisions; grandiose concepts and complex ideas lead to failure. Remember, you are asking prospective customers who don't care about you and know nothing about you to suddenly take an interest. Keep your assumptions grounded in your reality, and keep your action steps simple and practical.

Stop writing about selling and go sell something. There's no way to predict or prepare for every possible occurrence. Attempting to do so is a fool's errand. The more time you spend theorizing and imagining, the less time you'll actually spend executing and testing. And, yes, those lost minutes will add up fast. So just get it done; don't overplan. Every day that you don't make money is one more day you'll be unable to support your life burn rate. Don't set yourself up for failure with unachievable cut-off dates, but don't be afraid to remove yourself from your comfort zone. Set realistic timelines, stick to launch dates, and keep moving your start-up forward.

You're not a fortune-teller. Until you know for certain what your business actually is, how can you begin to predict what it will become? Planning for tomorrow instead of today will only ensure that there won't be a tomorrow. So forget the 10-year plan. Focus on the 10-day plan.

Successful entrepreneurs work to minimize and eliminate the need for unsubstantiated assumptions before setting long-term growth objectives. Get a few successful and unsuccessful yesterdays under your belt before you try to plan out any long-term tomorrows.

Financial projections are total nonsense. Before you claim that your start-up will earn $200 million in five years, try to earn $1 in a single month. The only thing 100 percent true, valid, or substantiated about your projected revenues and profits will be that they are undoubtedly wrong.

Leave your hockey stick projections on the ice. Unless you want to set yourself up for failure and high blood pressure, don't fool yourself into believing that you can create realistic milestones without spending a single day in the trenches. Instead, concentrate on minimizing expenses and mastering your selling techniques. Figure out how to generate income daily to support your life burn rate, not on some random annual figure. As your business develops, you might—and that's a *big* might—need financial forecasts for investors and banks. Should you be lucky enough to get to court the option of getting investment funds or a loan, at least you'll have real data on which to base your nonsensical projections.

THE ONE-PARAGRAPH START-UP PLAN

You probably think I'm a quack. There's absolutely no way you can write everything there is to know about your brilliant start-up in one paragraph, right?

Guess what? You're wrong. You don't have much to say—because you haven't proved a thing yet.

The *last* thing with which you should concern yourself now—during the earliest stages of your business—is writing lengthy plans or long-winded executive summaries. Perhaps someday there'll be a time when elongated materials are needed; I'm sure there will be hundreds of out-of-work MBAs dying for the chance to write that plan to validate their education. But now is not that moment.

Now is the time to kill the traditional business plan in favor of a real, practical tool.

The One-Paragraph Start-Up Plan is exactly what it sounds like: Your entire business concept boiled down into an easily digestible short, sweet, and to-the-point format. Unlike traditional business-planning methodologies that teach you to brainstorm-write-brainstorm-write-revise-revise-execute, the goal of the one-paragraph plan is to have you brainstorm-write-execute-revise-execute. There are fundamental differences between these two approaches. The traditional route would have you finalize your entire strategy based on a hypothesis without bothering to test or validate it. The One-Paragraph Start-Up Plan is designed to test your hypothesis through daily experimentation. It also serves as a fluid action strategy that grows along with your start-up.

It took me three days to research, brainstorm, and write my first One-Paragraph Start-Up Plan. On the fourth day, I was up and running. Was it the perfect plan? Not by a long shot. But it got me started in no time, and set me on a course to generate revenue immediately.

Eight questions to answer when crafting your first draft. Without breaking the previously outlined rules, answer each of the following eight questions completely and honestly—and in no more than one or two sentences. Put real thought into your answers, and feel confident that you can support and substantiate your core beliefs with relevant arguments.

1. What is the service your business performs or the product it provides today?
2. How does your business produce or provide the product or service right now?
3. How will customers use your product or service as it exists right now?
4. How will your business generate immediate revenue?
5. Who are the primary clients your business will target immediately?
6. How will you market your start-up to prospective clients with the resources you have at your direct disposal?
7. How are you different than your competitors right now?

8. What are the secondary and tertiary client bases you will target once you've attained success with your primary base?

Obviously, your first draft is not the final plan. Think of it as an outline for the beginning of your journey. As an example, check out my first One-Paragraph Start-Up Plan for my business, Sizzle It!, a specialized sizzle reel video production company.

Pre-Execution One-Paragraph Plan: Sizzle It!

Sizzle It! produces and edits sizzle reels, which are 3- to 5-minute promotional videos that combine video, graphics, photos, audio, and messaging to offer viewers a fast-paced, stylized overview of a product, service, or brand. The company's team of freelance editors edits together media materials submitted by its clients. Sizzle It!'s primary clients are boutique public relations firms. It produces revenue by charging these clients flat fees for editorial services. The company will focus its marketing efforts on cold calls, search engine optimization, and networking at public relations industry events. Unlike its diversified competitors that offer large service rosters, Sizzle It! will only focus on producing sizzle reels. The company will expand its client roster to include advertising agencies and small businesses.

Break your start-up plan into Guess and Checklists. Now it's time to turn your paragraph into a functional, action-based plan that you can revise regularly. A Guess and Checklist is a series of action steps designed to get your company up, running, and executing immediately. The goal of the exercise is to field-test each of your assumptions and determine whether they are true, false, or incomplete. As you learn lessons from your successes, failures, and nonstarters along your journey, you can then modify your plan to make it a formula for success.

Begin by breaking down each sentence in your plan into five steps you can execute immediately—actionable statements you can convert into reality. List each action step chronologically in a checklist format; it's no different than a to-do list or a series of task reminders in your mobile phone or computer. Include applicable deadlines and denote any related expenses. In Chapter 8 on shoestrapping, I will teach you how to minimize start-up expenses and work with a shoestring budget. But for now, just determine what you think the expense will be and write it down. Take a look at how I broke down one of the sentences in my start-up plan into five action steps (including the deadlines I set for completing each item):

Sentence: *Sizzle It!'s primary clients are boutique public relations firms.*

1. Create a list of all boutique public relation firms in NYC. 1/25/08
2. Research contact information for each firm. 1/28/08
3. Contact each prospective client to set up introductory meetings. 2/15/08
4. Produce a company video reel for presentations. 2/15/08 ($200)
5. During meetings with prospective clients, offer a one-time discount of 50 percent off their first sizzle reel purchase.

Make sure that all of your action steps will move your business forward in some way. Even still, I promise you that there will be many improvements to come.

Do your action steps yield fruit? Once you compose the first drafts of your Guess and Checklists for each sentence in your One-Paragraph Start-Up Plan, it's time to get to work.

Execute each action step as completely as possible. Keep your Guess and Checklists with you at all times—either on a mobile device or a printout—and jot down quick notes whenever you learn something new.

Once each task is completed, evaluate your findings with these six questions:

1. What worked and what didn't?
2. What was the result of each action step?
3. Was the overall experience positive or negative? Why?
4. What did you learn during the process?
5. Which steps can be modified or improved for better results? How?
6. Which steps need to be deleted all together?

In the case of Sizzle It!, executing my various action steps quickly opened my eyes to many things I couldn't have known prior to execution. For example, cold-calling PR professionals proved worthless; however, my search engine optimization tactics were raking in the dough. Though I managed to find a good amount of contact names at PR firms, I soon realized that the only useful ones were those of brand managers and senior account executives. Our 50 percent discount for first-time clients was a total flop. My research led me to find hundreds of independent PR specialists—a whole new grouping of prospective clients that I wasn't aware of previously. These discoveries—as well as several others—allowed me to fine-tune and strengthen every aspect of my start-up. By doing so, my results improved week after week.

True, false, or incomplete? Based on the information you gathered while executing your Guess and Checklist, determine if your original hypothesis is true, false, or incomplete. In the case of the Sizzle It! example, my original thesis was both false and incomplete. Not only did I miss an entire client category, I also failed to research the right decision makers. Sometimes you'll validate your hypothesis; in other cases, you'll see that you were totally off base. Whatever the outcome, identify and plug the holes in your false or incomplete assertions.

Create your success formulas. Scrap what failed and improve on minor successes to bolster home runs. Adjust your plan to account for ways in which you can begin to transform each of your flawed assertions into true and complete statements. Use your findings to create new, more educated insights and craft more in-depth, specific checklists. Repeat this process regularly until your hypotheses turn into facts.

Two months of actively guessing and checking this particular Sizzle It! hypothesis allowed me to produce a proven marketing, sales, and referral formula that our sales team still uses today. Here is my revised One-Paragraph Start-Up Plan sentence and its corresponding Guess and Checklist with the five amended action steps.

Sentence: *Sizzle It!'s primary clients are independent PR specialists and brand managers and senior account executives at boutique and midsize public relations firms.*

1. Research the names and contact information for brand managers and senior account executives at boutique public relations firms, as well as independent PR specialists. (Monday)
2. E-mail each of these individuals with an offer for a free breakfast or lunch in a forum of their choosing in exchange for an introductory meeting. (Monday–Wednesday, $50)
3. Use meetings as an opportunity to exhibit the company's three-minute sizzle reel and demo the company's client tools on SizzleIt.com.

4. At the end of meetings with prospective clients, offer them a free year's supply of coffee with their first purchase. ($200)

5. Two days after each meeting, e-mail the prospective client an offer for a free breakfast for their entire office in exchange for successful client referrals. ($150)

Always look for ways to improve your Guess and Checklists. Doing so will keep you on top of your game and allow you to produce a series of definable, stepped-out blueprints for each and every part of your business.

Formulate and prove new hypotheses regularly. Just because you prove out all of your original premises doesn't mean that you're done and on your way to easy street.

In fact, this is only the beginning.

Over the years, constantly questioning and improving on my One-Paragraph Start-Up Plan has led Sizzle It! to become a profitable, scalable company that is poised for strong growth in various new markets.

Post-Execution One-Paragraph Plan: Sizzle It!

Sizzle It! produces and edits sizzle reels, which are 3- to 5-minute promotional and demo videos that combine video, graphics, photos, audio, and messaging to offer viewers a fast-paced, stylized overview of a product, service, or brand. Sizzle reels are produced for, or incorporated into, B-to-B sales presentations, product demonstrations, training videos, online media campaigns, and electronic press kits. Sizzle It!'s primary clients include independent PR specialists, and brand managers and senior account executives at boutique public relations firms and marketing agencies, and conference event planners. It produces revenue by charging these clients flat and hourly fees for production and editorial services. The company markets to customers using e-mail marketing, search engine optimization, and networking at public relations industry events. Sizzle It! gives away a free year's supply of coffee as a gift to each of its new clients. Unlike competitors, Sizzle It! is the only video editorial company that solely focuses on producing sizzle reels. Additionally, the company offers customers access to an online client portal that strengthens their abilities to manage their projects and brings transparency to the production process. Sizzle It! will expand its client roster to include creative directors at advertising agencies, entrepreneurs in small businesses, brand managers in product companies, and the hosts, actors, and spokespeople behind personality-driven brands.

I wasn't kidding when I told you that this One-Paragraph Start-Up Plan was a living, breathing plan that holds a symbiotic relationship with your business. And if it dies, your business may not be far behind.

Never get comfortable. Always strive to improve your existing statements, add new client bases, and prove new hypotheses. Continue to sharpen your entrepreneurial skills. In time, you will be able to better hypothesize from the get-go, shortening the time frame it takes to complete and prove your success formulas.

6

TO PARTNER OR NOT TO PARTNER

Whether you're looking for a business partner, a mentor, a lawyer, or an accountant, it is vital that you separate the lions from the vultures. Nothing demonstrates this point more than my experience working with another multimedia start-up (this was before *the company that shalt not be named*). This particular company's demise was brought on by one of its majority shareholders and managers—or, as I refer to him, Mr. CEO.

Mr. CEO was the perfect storm of incompetence, egotism, and poor decision-making abilities. To sum him up in a nutshell, he loved ordering people around, driving an expensive sports car, and telling anyone who spoke to him for more than 30 seconds that he was, indeed, a CEO. Never mind that the company he pretended to run was worth less than the paper on which his fancy business cards were printed. In fact, the only thing he *didn't* seem to like was real work.

During his inglorious two-year tenure, Mr. CEO:

- Carelessly spent more than $400,000 without earning a penny of revenue.
- Charged expensive "client" dinner meetings on the company credit card regularly.
- "Worked from home" three or more days per week, checked his e-mail only once per day, and referred to Fridays as "Hot Tub Day."
- Misrepresented and exaggerated our products' capabilities on a daily basis, thereby forcing us to scramble to back up his faulty promises.

- Hired a technology company that specialized in military and defense products to build our tween-focused Web site. The vendor burned through $40,000, missed every deadline, and never delivered a final product.

In the end, Mr. CEO blamed the company's failure on everyone but himself. He cried about how his partner didn't do enough, bitched about how the employees didn't cut it, and swore that the start-up would have made it if it weren't so severely undercapitalized. However, although there was certainly blame to go around, our team could only be as effective as its leadership—and our leadership had failed us.

You should not take lightly the decision to partner with another individual or company. Nor should partnering be the result of enthusiasm, spontaneity, or a "gut feeling." Partnerships can turn out to be a blessing or a curse. For every thriving relationship, there are thousands that end up stagnant, dissolving, dysfunctional, or worse—in court. I've worked alongside many workhorses, and I've been victim to blood-sucking ticks. For each brilliant advisor from whom I benefited greatly, I was cannibalized by a greedy shark. In almost every instance of the latter, I would have been able to separate the winners from the losers early on and kick the garbage to the curb before I was hung out to dry—if I had only performed basic due diligence at the beginning.

Much like marriage—for better or worse, for richer or for poorer, through good times and bad, and as long as your business shall live—you will be attached to your partner at the hip, 24/7. So before you tie the knot at a shotgun wedding, you'll need to rate individuals like they're Olympic figure skaters. Most won't even make it to the qualification rounds; few will even get the chance to try out. And select few, if any, will ever win gold. But those who survive your sharpest scrutiny and most severe due diligence will truly deserve it when you finally proclaim, "I do."

THE WORST PARTNERS FOR YOUR START-UP

To err is human. To partner with flawed, damaged people is just plain stupid. If you surround yourself with idiots and don't realize they're idiots, guess what: The only *real* idiot is you. Before you hand over your life savings and social security number to someone else, you must be sure that you're not giving equity or authority to a complete and total buffoon destined to take you through the ringer.

Here are some archetypes and personalities that will make for absolutely disastrous partnerships. Avoid these miscreants like the plague. And if some of these morons remind you of yourself, shape up or ship out.

Mr. Procrastinator needs every "i" to be dotted and "t" to be crossed before he schedules an official product launch date. He enjoys researching competitors, building industry case studies, and improving his 150-page business plan. Mr. Procrastinator really wanted the new business to be up and running by now, but still feels something isn't *quite* right. He plans on putting together another comprehensive survey to send to all of his colleagues, friends, and family in the next few weeks to help flesh out the concept further.

Excuses should not be tolerated. A good plan today is always better than a perfect plan tomorrow. Steer clear of excuse-prone procrastinators; instead, seek out self-starters who run with the ball and make things happen.

Ms. Employee is a first-time entrepreneur with a pristine resume and an abundance of references. She enjoys collecting a weekly paycheck, health benefits, and eating dinner with her family every night promptly at 7 PM. Unfortunately, Ms. Employee isn't really self-sufficient and doesn't know how to move the business forward without you instructing her on every single move. Plus if your investment deal doesn't pan out soon, she's going to need to find a real job to pay the kids' college tuitions.

Risk-averse individuals who do not share your priorities will not be productive partners. Don't work with people who cannot commit the same amount of time, energy, and financial resources as you.

Mr. College Buddy had a stroke of genius while out at the bar one night, wrote it on a cocktail napkin, and asked you to help him "make it happen." He enjoys bragging about his great idea and giving you directions on how to execute (because he's not really into the "heavy lifting" thing). The issue is that he's moving across country to start med school in the fall. But fear not—Mr. College Buddy will make himself available by phone when he's not studying, working, in class, or on a date. And he'll be sure to forward you the address where you can mail his 50 percent of the profits.

Never assume all of the risk in exchange for half the reward. Ideas are worthless without execution. Before you bring a coconceived idea to fruition, make certain that your partner plans to be around for the long haul.

Ms. Inventor thinks she's created the next billion-dollar widget. She enjoys giving two-hour dissertations on Chinese electrical engineering standards to investors and making business decisions based on "nice people" and "gut feelings." Ms. Inventor doesn't really understand the phrase "in the black," but feels it's imperative to spend all of the company's investment proceeds on research and development.

Brilliant academics do not necessarily make brilliant business people. Make sure that your partner understands the difference between theory and reality, has her feet on the ground, and isn't a robot disguised as a human being.

Mr. Always Right will be the first person to tell you that he is never wrong. His favorite phrase is "my way or the highway."

He will rarely discuss his decision-making process, because he views such discussions as a weakness. He enjoys demeaning any partners who don't agree with him, and making vital decisions without telling them. Funny thing about Mr. Right: He always seems to blame everyone but himself when his plans don't pan out—and he actually turns out to be wrong.

Communication is the key to a successful partnership. Find a collaborator, not a dictator. No one is *always* right.

Ms. Dreamer will say this line a lot: "One day, when we're millionaires . . . " She loves talking about retiring by 29 and imagining how she'll spend her hypothetical millions on a gold-plated yacht that she'll dock off the coast of her private island. One small problem with Ms. Dreamer: She doesn't seem to know how to keep the business above water from month to month.

Big paydays come from years of hard work and persistence, not excessive rambling and daydreaming. It's important that your partner be both positive and optimistic, but it is equally important that she be grounded and focused.

Mr. Spender can't possibly survive without a six-figure salary, lavish office, and an in-house cigar roller. Price is no object when it comes to entertaining a client or flying first class. If you're lucky, Mr. Spender might even invite you to one of the extravagant dinner meetings that he charges on your company's corporate card.

I cannot emphasize it enough: There is *no such thing* as an unlimited checkbook. Team up with fiscally conservative, financially responsible individuals who strive to make every dollar benefit your company's growth and development, not their personal lifestyles.

Ms. Vacation seems nice enough. I'd tell you more about Ms. Vacation, but I don't know much about her. She never seems to be around.

No-shows are deadweights who eat away profits. Only work with people who will strive to earn breaks—not those who feel entitled to them.

Mr. Personal Issues goes by many names, including Mr. Broke or Mr. Poor Me. He always has a sad story to tell. On the same day as your company's keynote presentation at the big conference, his son's wisdom teeth needed to be pulled and his dog died of pneumonia. He would love to attend next week's investor meeting, but he's probably going to be tied up all day at his divorce hearing. Unfortunately, Mr. Personal Issues can't afford his legal bills, so he'll need to pull a little more money out of the company this month to keep his ex-wife from taking 50 percent of his equity in the settlement. But he promises that this will be the *last* time he needs money . . . really.

You're not in business to be a babysitter or a psychiatrist. If a potential partner seems to have a few screws loose, run as fast as you can in the other direction.

DON'T CONSIDER LETTING WORTHLESS FLAKY PEOPLE TRY OUT

This mnemonic device is one of my favorites; I use it to qualify prospective partners, advisors, or teammates. My phrase—"Don't Consider Letting Worthless Flaky People Try Out"—represents the following seven-item checklist:

1. Dependability
2. Character
3. Loyalty
4. Work ethic
5. Finances
6. Personal issues
7. Trust

These quality tests will assess your prospective partners' personalities and character traits, and help you to determine whether they are the right fits for your entrepreneurial endeavors.

Dependability. Someone who isn't dependable will be a detriment to both your own and your company's reputation. When you consider whether you can rely on someone, ask yourself questions that put his or her level of commitment and steadfastness into perspective. Would this person put the start-up before personal matters? Can he or she get the job done with or without you in a similar fashion and timeline as you could? Will that person be around today, tomorrow, and 10 years from now? If something happened to you, would your business flourish and thrive—or crumble under your partner's leadership?

Never bind yourself to people who are inconsistent, unpredictable, or erratic; otherwise, no one will be around to help you hang your "Going Out of Business" sign.

Character. Finding smart, dependable, and trustworthy partners is only half the battle. If their personalities clash with yours at every turn, you'll be able to clock your divorce with an egg timer. Study each of your candidate's character traits and habits. Are you long lost brothers or polar opposites? Which of his or her qualities are complimentary to yours, if any? Which can't you stand? Do any make your blood boil? Can you stand the thought of sitting in a room with this person for 24 hours? Would you even care to try?

Before you sign on the dotted line make sure you can happily visualize working side by side with your partner every day for years to come. Don't work with anyone who makes you want to swing from the rafters, dangling from a rope. (After all, it's quite difficult for a busy entrepreneur to find the time to run a business while hatching a scheme to make a murder look like an accident.)

Loyalty. Plain and simple—you can't buy loyalty. And if someone's is for sale, they're about as loyal as a hungry rabies-infested dog looking for a meal. Determine whether your potential partner is more likely to look out for your combined interests or merely his own. When times get tough, will this person be shoulder-to-shoulder with you or duck and run for cover? Will he or she be by your side to the bitter end—or stab you in the back?

The last thing you want to do is end up in a sketchy partnership without reciprocated loyalty. This can lead your so-called "partners" to take advantage of your good graces. If you even have the slightest of hesitations about where your candidate's loyalties lie, kick him to the curb before he has a chance to hurt you.

Work ethic. Does your candidate work hard or hardly work? Obviously, there's a big difference. Will the individual be as passionate, persistent, and dedicated to your business as you are? Does he back up the talk with one hell of a walk; or does the hour of the day or day of the week dictate his level of commitment to the cause? Is he or she an outgoing self-starter who will push you harder, or an unmotivated handholder who will slow you down? Is this individual always ready to get his or her hands dirty, or do certain tasks seem to be "beneath" him? Does he or she believe that now is always better than later and does he or she know the difference between business and busy-ness?

If someone isn't likely to be beside you in the trenches—fighting every battle with every ounce of his being—boot him out of the foxhole before he gets you shot.

Finances. Knowing your prospective partner's credit score, financial status, and fiscal past are vital to predicting your potential partnership's economic health. Does the person live frugally or extravagantly? Is he or she a spender or a saver? Does he have a lot of debt or liabilities? Do you have similar savings and financial resources at your disposals, or totally uneven net worths? Does the person know how to spend money smartly and effectively, or does she have a history of pissing it away?

You and your partner will be the bankroll and financial backbone of your business. For that reason, you need to be able to support company initiatives in both good times and bad. Make sure that the person with whom you partner is completely honest about her financial picture and provides data to support her claims. Don't get stuck with the bill. If you aren't comfortable cosigning on a corporate credit card or you determine that you'll be the only financial lifeline to which your company has access, then walk away—and take your credit score with you.

Personal issues. Know everything there is to know about your prospective partner's life before you enter a partnership with him. In what stage of life is your candidate? Is it similar to yours or entirely different? Is he married with children, and/or have a healthy home life? Does he or she suffer from any debilitating addictions such as drugs, gambling, or alcohol? Will the individual's personal life affect the company, its finances, or its reputation?

True partners must be able to talk about *everything*—without hesitation. Be sure that you're ending up with a basket of joy and not a basket case. Do a full background check and discuss every imaginable topic—from business to politics to family life—with your prospective partner.

Trust. Trust is *the* most vital piece of the partnership puzzle. Without it, you have nothing between you. Break down your levels of trust into degrees of severity when ascertaining someone's reliability, starting with small offenses and ending with the most serious deal breakers. Would you trust this person to watch your pet? How about your home? What about your spouse, significant other, or child? Would you lend the person $100? Would you tell them your bank account password or ATM pin number?

Do not sugarcoat your trust questions. You are putting your well-being and future in the hands of another individual—so you must be *absolutely certain* that this person can be trusted with that responsibility. There mustn't be a shadow of a doubt

Have "The Talk"

Sit down with your potential partner in a room, turn off your cell phones, put away your computers, and lock the door. Before you become blood brothers (or sisters), you must openly and honestly discuss each of the 10 topics below in detail to ensure that you are the right fit and on the same page.

Listen carefully to the responses. Any answers that seem unclear, incomplete, half-assed, or so brief that your potential partner appears to be hiding something should immediately set off red flags in your head. Unresponsive answers such as "none of your business" or "I don't know" should set off sirens and launch fireworks. Who knows? By the end of your talk, maybe your partner candidate won't want to partner with *you!*

1. What debt or financial obligations do each of you have?
2. What information would be revealed about each of you in background and credit checks?
3. What are both of your religious views, political affiliations, bad habits, and working styles?
4. What personal, educational, business, or third-party obligations, if any, will take each of you away from your company responsibilities? How regularly and for how long will these commitments be factors?
5. In your business bank account, how much of the money would each of you spend and how much of it would you save?
6. Do either of you have any open legal disputes, past personal or corporate legal issues, or potential legal issues that may come out of the woodwork at some point? If so, what potential ramifications do each of you and/or the business face?
7. How would you like to structure the partnership in terms of equity, capital outlay, and other such deal points?

(*continued*)

(continued)

8. What do you expect from the company and the partnership? What are your goals and objectives for the business?

9. What situations and circumstances—both business and personal—would lead to each of you wanting to end the partnership?

10. If any of the answers to these questions were proven false or incomplete, what actions would you expect your partner to take and what consequences would you expect?

---

that if a rock were falling off the cliff and you were standing underneath that your partner would push you out of the way or trade his life for yours. If you believe there's a chance he'd stand idly by, walk away before a boulder has the chance to crush you.

NEVER JUMP RIGHT IN: THE WATER'S NOT FINE

People who dive headfirst into partnerships because it "feels right" are, quite honestly, morons. When you consider others' needs before your own or think with your heart instead of your brain, your warm and fuzzy feelings are sure to trick you into entering into a miserable partnership. Just because you've managed to find an individual who survived your most intense examination doesn't mean it's time to hold hands and leap into the deep end together—that is, if you don't want to drown.

Before you move forward, there are five big questions you need to ask yourself:

1. **Do I really need a partner at all?** Weigh all the pros and the cons of taking on a partner. What can a partner do for your business that you can't? Are there ways to fill the knowledge or talent gaps without taking on a fellow

shareholder? Can you replace the need for a partner by, for example, hiring an outsourced third party? Consider all of the alternatives before moving forward. Remember, once you give your equity away, it might be gone forever.

2. **Are there other mutually beneficial options besides a standard partnership?** If your potential collaborator invented an amazing gizmo but has less practical business knowledge than a Chia Pet, getting stuck with him could very well hamper your ability to execute the company strategy as you see fit. However, that doesn't mean you both can't prosper from your individual strengths. Before gulping down the partner Kool-Aid, look into suitable substitutes such as licensing deals, joint ventures, or strategic partnerships and see if it makes better business sense to keep other people's hands off your equity.

3. **Do I need this partner?** Would you be able to unequivocally defend your partnership decision to your strongest critic? Are you partnering with this individual for the right reasons? Does he or she undeniably add value to the business? Are your collective skills complimentary or redundant? What tangible assets and resources does the other person bring to the table? Are your short-term and long-term goals in sync? And finally, in the best of all worlds, is this individual the best possible partner for your start-up? Answer these questions as truthfully as possible. If you aren't completely satisfied with your responses, then don't settle down with your candidate. Walk away until you find the right fit. Partnering with someone despite your reservations is a terrible decision, and is guaranteed to put the future of your start-up in jeopardy.

4. **Are you absolutely certain that the partnership works for both parties, in both theory and execution?** Live together for a while before you get hitched. Test it out.

Determine some achievable milestones and focus on accomplishing those goals together. This will give you time to see how the roles in the partnership will be structured. In my experience, most partnerships show signs of failure in days or weeks, not months or years; so you'll know relatively quickly if you've met the "partner of your dreams."

5. **Do you have the agreement locked down?** Your partnership document must define the roles each partner will play, as well as outline equity ownership, corporate responsibilities, voting powers, and how company stock can be bought or sold. During the honeymoon phase, it can be hard to imagine a world that isn't filled with champagne wishes and caviar dreams. However, in dire times, fear and anger can quickly turn your best friends into your worst enemies. Shit happens. Be protected. "He said, she said" claims will not hold up in court—and that napkin you signed over a beer won't be so legally binding if your one-time partner in crime sues you for everything you've got.

PART III

FROM THE
GROUND UP

7

ACT LIKE A START-UP, STUPID

The original concept behind the *company that shalt not be named* was pretty straightforward:

To combine marketing and creative media to produce exciting and targeted solutions that generate results for our clients across all mediums.

Simple enough, right? However, my partners and I were so concerned with making our start-up into the "next big thing" that we completely lost sight of our core principles. What we created ended up being nothing more than smoke and mirrors held together by hopes and dreams.

We effectively transformed our unproven, unprofitable media production company into a money pit creative agency/technology firm/investment company that sought out clients who had no money either:

Company X is the premier one-stop-shop venture management company, with a primary concentration on media-based start-up enterprises. Our mission is to combine multichannel marketing, creative media, and innovative technology to offer start-up enterprises exciting, inventive, and consumer-specific solutions that generate or enhance topline revenue growth. After conducting comprehensive due diligence, our Company will select clients with minimal financial resources and offer them a wide array of multidiscipline media and business development services. Since marketing and media costs are extremely prohibitive for start-ups, we will provide strategic services to its clients in exchange for gross revenue sharing opportunities.

Now *there's* a mouthful of crap for you to swallow.

So how did we let this happen? How did we take something so simple and convolute it to such an absurd level? Several reasons:

- We failed to act, think, or operate like a start-up.
- We arbitrarily altered our course each time we became discouraged.
- We had screwed-up priorities.
- We never laid the proper groundwork for sustainable success.
- No part of our start-up was automated, systemized, or simplified.
- Our thinking was too conventional and traditional.
- We focused on overscaled growth, even though we could barely handle our current size.

Building a business is like constructing a house. If you don't take time to lay a solid, sturdy foundation, the whole structure is doomed to come crashing down around you. Putting the right protocols, systems, and thought processes in place in the early stages of your start-up will reduce the chances of your roof caving in.

Now it's time to teach you how to act, think, and operate like a start-up to ensure that your house won't collapse around you.

SURVIVING A "REAL" DAY IN THE LIFE

There is absolutely nothing glorious or glamorous about starting a business. Don't let the lifestyles of the rock star entrepreneurs or reality TV fool you. Forget about fancy offices, fast cars, and fat expense accounts. That level of success is rare and never built overnight. In most cases, it takes decades.

While launching a start-up is undoubtedly an exciting and liberating experience, managing the organization on a daily basis can be anything but a dream. If you let your visions of "the life" blind your good sense, you'll find yourself disappointed and looking to quit with every misstep.

The entrepreneur's lifestyle is not 9-to-5. Entrepreneurship is both a lifestyle and a state of mind. Becoming a business owner means that you're becoming more than a person. The goal is to form a symbiotic relationship with your business—in effect, *becoming* your business.

Though the entrepreneurial lifestyle can be truly rewarding, you will only get out of it what you put into it. So give yourself completely to the cause. Reassess and rearrange your priorities. Figure out what's truly important, and abandon what isn't.

Need to work late hours? Do it!

Have to do grunt work to save cash? Hurry up and get it done!

Need to downgrade your lifestyle to accommodate your cash flow? Well, what are you waiting for?

That being said, don't become an entrepreneurial martyr. The term "start-up" refers to the earliest phase of a business's life cycle; it's not where your business is meant to stay for all eternity. Every aspect of your company's success will fall solely on your shoulders during its earliest stages, but this working methodology will be heavily taxing on your body, mind, and soul. It is not sustainable, and at some point, it will work against—rather than for—your business growth. Again, this is why it's imperative that you work your ass off to get out of this developmental stage as quickly as possible. You want to get to the point where you can hire people and transition from being dependent on bus passes and chicken noodle soup into a stable business owner who works on—not in—his business.

Rise above the grind. Entrepreneurs can't afford to see the world through rose-color glasses. You won't be chauffeured in private black cars, no one will think you're important, and rarely will you spearhead life-altering meetings. Chances are you'll spend most days working out of your apartment, sending out countless introductory e-mails to prospective clients, and rationing takeout into multiple meals.

The reality is that the world is an unfair, unpredictable and full of hard knocks place where a day without a sale is one day closer to bankruptcy. There will be good days when you'll feel like you're king of the world and bad days where you'll want to crawl up into the fetal position in a dark corner. There will be moments of victory followed by weakness, doubt, and defeat; times when you feel as though you can't even think about your start-up for another second. You'll undoubtedly fall down and won't want to—or think you can't—get back up. If you truly want to become a stable and successful self-employed business owner who lives on her own terms, there is only one thing I can say to you.

It's your choice: Accept the entrepreneurial lifestyle for what it really is or go find a "real" job where you'll never truly reap the benefits of your labor.

Don't just sit there crying or looking for sympathy when things aren't going your way; instead, figure out how to get back on track. If you find yourself in a dark hole because cash flow is drying up, dig yourself out by bootstrapping, and improving your marketing and sales tactics. If times get tough because of the economy, restrategize your price structure, retool your service offering to make sense under the conditions, and push forward with a new sales campaign geared to spin a negative moment into a positive bottom line.

Your days won't be easy, especially in the beginning. However, if you work hard with passion and purpose, they'll certainly be more fulfilling, rewarding, and fruitful than any "real" job. Never forget why you decided to become an entrepreneur in the first place. Many times, those convictions will serve as the only light at the end of the tunnel.

There is an "I" in team. As president, CEO, and chief bottle washer, you can expect to wear many hats; most of which you've never worn before or never even thought you'd try on. Perhaps this will be your first time writing a client proposal, or

Ten Ways to Avoid Quitting or Failure in Your First Three Months

1. **Amass clients, not capital.** Don't sell a business idea to people who won't care—sell products and services to people who *might* care. Fund your company on consumer revenues and build your business with *only* your business in mind—not hypothetical future investors.
2. **Sell! Sell! Sell!** Concentrate on selling—not planning—the plan. Create income, not paperwork.
3. **Perfection is the enemy.** Good enough is better than perfect. Forget crossing your t's and dotting your i's; your priority is to find the fastest routes to generate immediate cash flow.
4. **Productivity at all costs.** Stay organized and efficient, but don't get caught up in busy work. If your tasks aren't directly related to your bottom line, scrap them in favor of efforts that are.
5. **Automate, delegate, or outsource remedial tasks.** Automate tasks you can't scrap (like paying bills and bookkeeping) with online tools and cheap services so you can keep your eye on the revenue-generating tasks.
6. **Be penny wise, not dollar foolish.** Always attempt to save money wherever and whenever possible. However, don't try to save money at the expense of productivity as your start-up begins to generate positive cash flow; rather, invest in productivity when necessary to increase your effectiveness. Outsourcing select activities (such as those mentioned in number 5) will dramatically free up your time and keep your attention where it needs to be: on sales and marketing.
7. **Be realistic.** Stay reasonable and grounded. Keep your sales, marketing, and business growth assumptions and

expectations in check. It's better to surprise yourself with positive results than it is to consistently disappoint yourself with negative ones.

8. **Fix it as it breaks.** If something isn't working, determine the root cause, assess the possible solutions, and fix it—right then and there. Don't make the same mistakes twice, or the second time might be your last mistake.

9. **Don't be a procrastinator.** Tomorrow is *never* better than today. Wake up every morning knowing how you are going to get the most out of your day. Get off your ass and find ways to make money.

10. **Connect with people who know what you don't.** You don't know all, nor should you try to. Find mentors who can answer your questions, help you move your business out of ditches, and set you straight when you're being a moron.

---

figuring out how to shoot a video for your Web site. Either way, my point is that some hats will fit right away—and others won't fit at all. For those that aren't so snug, fear not. You'll figure it out. How am I so sure? Because in the beginning you have *no choice* but to figure it out. If you don't do it, it won't get done.

From photocopying to paying bills to cold calling, you'll need to do *everything* in the earliest stages of your start-up. Don't expect to be able to hire an assistant or intern right away; many times, you'll have to do grunt work. Yes, it's important to win bids for service contracts, but it's equally important that you remember to fax the client an agreement, follow up on the status of unpaid invoices, and collect your fees.

No matter how remedial, unpleasant, or boring a task may be, you'll have to master each process in your business from the bottom up—until you have the means to outsource, delegate, or eliminate them. If you're a plumber, you need to be able to fix a toilet before you can teach an employee to do it in a manner to your standards. If you're a childcare provider, it would behoove you not to work with the loudest or messiest kids; how else would you be able to teach your future employees how to handle such kids? Don't let your ego and delicate sensibilities get in the way of getting things done. Do whatever it takes to be successful with your own two hands. The faster you grow your company on your own back, the quicker you'll have access to more hands, options, and resources.

If you feel stumped or lost, take a deep breath, step back, and figure it out. Good advice and answers are always available; you just need to know who to ask, where to look, and be able to sift out the gold from the dirt.

Though entrepreneurship certainly isn't easy, it's not all that complicated either. At its very core, going into business for one's self is the process of selling something to someone else. That's it. Whenever you feel overwhelmed, calm yourself down by remembering that simple fact—and get back to basics.

Always sweat the small stuff. The smallest, seemingly insignificant issues have a funny way of snowballing into major disasters. Little blips on the radar once deemed unimportant may actually be warning signs of dangers on the horizon. For example, dismissing a cash-flow problem as the result of a slow, off-peak month—rather than further investigating to determine if your collections process is too lenient or your services are priced too low—might lead to real problems down the road.

Failure should never be an option if you were able to see it coming. Check each area of your business regularly. Look for improvements and work to fine-tune every element. Identify the real problems behind the small stuff before you find yourself getting ruined by the big stuff.

Win the war, not just a battle. Entrepreneurship is a daily game of kill or be killed, with high stakes: your livelihood and your future. For every triumph, there may be 10 defeats. There may be many rejections before your first sale. Lessons learned from a series of failed marketing tactics might be the reason you score big with a later, more informed campaign. Some days, you'll take five steps backward for every step forward. However—at the risk of sounding cliché—it's true that whatever doesn't kill you only makes you stronger.

Mental fortitude and persistence are the keys to prevailing over adversity. Never retreat in the face of hardship or let the game kill you. Even the most successful entrepreneurs suffer sales and marketing setbacks and resistant marketplaces. Play to win instead. Find the balls you didn't know you had and attack obstacles—and your competition—head on with only one mission in mind: complete and total annihilation.

Remember, it's not how you fall down that defines you, but how fast and strong you get back up.

GET YOUR HEAD IN THE GAME, CHUMP

Successful entrepreneurs aren't just experts at strategy and execution. They've also mastered the art of communication, winning over skeptics, and positioning their companies against others.

Achieving success requires that you properly prepare yourself to engage in daily psychological warfare. Everything about you and your business must be designed to maximize and control the flow of information and inspire others to act in your favor.

Make your own luck. Luck plays a major role in every business; however, that doesn't mean you should sit around and wait for good fortune to knock on your door. It will never just *show up*. You need to search it out.

Get fired up!

From what you wear to how you act, you must be a walking, talking billboard who is comfortable with marketing your business—and yourself. Convey your message and brand image with everything you do. You need not be a meek little mouse, but take care not to irritate people with overly excessive self-praise or used car salesman–type enthusiasm.

Don't sit at a desk all day; get out into the world! Be a scrappy and resilient self-starter with infectious energy and passion. Strike up random conversations. Join new social circles. Participate in business meet-ups and activities with like-minded people. Be a creative networker. I once attended a crowded marketer-networking event wearing a T-shirt with the phrase: INTRODUCE YOURSELF & I'LL GIVE YOU $1. That shirt attracted attention and earned me conversations with other guests. I was able to turn a $62 investment into five clients and thousands of dollars in revenue.

Make your own luck by hustling every day. You never know whom you'll meet or what you'll experience until you consistently put yourself out there.

Trust everyone, but always cut the deck. Many people will say they want to work with you. Others will promise you everything under the sun. But talk is cheap. Rarely will anyone be looking to do you some big favor for nothing in return. From "guaranteeing" results they can't provide to overcharging you for mediocre services, wolves in sheep's clothing will try to take advantage of you every step of the way. Never forget that everyone you meet will always put his own interests before yours.

Trust must be earned, not given.

My friend once hired a freelance Web designer he found from an ad on an online job board. The ad promised that said Web designer could build a professional-looking Web site in less than one week for $300. Two weeks later, there was still no Web site. The designer was in fact a con artist who knew nothing about Web design and disappeared with my friend's money.

Don't fall for unsubstantiated claims. Keep your guard up. When it comes to judging character, trust your gut. If you have a bad feeling or the slightest hesitation about someone's integrity or motives, say thanks but no thanks and walk away without looking back.

Bait more than one hook. Your product or service may be responsible for reeling in the fish, but you're in charge of setting the bait.

Do your due diligence on prospects before scheduled appointments and meetings. Conduct online background checks on all involved parties, and use this information to develop the bait based on the common ground you share with each individual. Similar hobbies, philanthropic interests, and business ambitions are a few bait examples.

Always keep an interesting conversation topic in your back pocket for chance encounters—and not one that starts with something as trivial and contrived as, "Do you believe this weather we're having?"

Don't look like you're *trying* to get a conversation going; just use a normal, relevant starting point to kick things off. Devise a series of conversation starters that will help you break the ice in any situation. Become a generalist. Don't just know about your own industry; learn others as well. Know what is going on in your local community and the world at large.

What's in it for you? You never know when a conversation can lead to new clients or revenue for your business. Sure, your business shouldn't be the first thing you talk about *every* time you start a conversation. However, it should be the first thing on your mind. Having a conversation with a used car salesman might not seem like a natural fit for your SAT prep tutoring service at first, but should you find out his wife is the local high school's principal and his daughter is about to start her college search, the used car salesman you almost wrote off just might be a client or referrer in your midst.

Small talk will get you nowhere fast. Always look for noninvasive methods of getting what you want from every

Gage the Potential of Every Conversation

Use this five-question checklist to figure out the possible benefits of every encounter from the start:

1. Are there any key phrases popping out at you that would make you assume this person is a relevant target or lead generator?
2. What does this individual's look, attitude, demeanor, and the conversation's subject matter tell you about her potential interest in your business?
3. Based on the conversation, what is the most likely outcome of this conversation—a sale, a referral, or nothing?
4. Is the best course of action to try to unlock immediate potential or set the bait for future gains?
5. Do you offer anything valuable to the individual that can help you get what you need from him in exchange?

encounter. Find ways to steer the conversation to a topic of your choosing. Use your situation, surroundings, or the prospect's chosen topics as an opening to steer the conversation. Whenever possible, find a way to help the person solve a problem—even if it's not related to your business in any way. If appropriate, get the person's contact information at the end of the conversation so you can follow up. Don't just trust an individual to call you or e-mail you because you handed the person a business card.

Master your poker face. Communication is 10 percent what you say, 20 percent how you say it, and 70 percent body language while you say it. Perception is reality. Just because your business is a small fish in a big pond doesn't mean you can't find ways to convey the same confidence and reliability as the big guys.

You may be a one-person wrecking crew behind the scenes—but no one will care whether your products come from a factory or a makeshift assembly line in your garage, as long as they arrive at their destination on time, on budget, and of the quality promised.

Never give away the real size of your company. Use "we" phrases instead of saying "I" or "me." Opt for team-oriented titles such as managing partner or principal instead of CEO or president. Create custom e-mail accounts by using your Web site's URL for company e-mail addresses rather than the generic Gmail, Hotmail, and Yahoo! accounts. Use multiple e-mail addresses for different departments such as techsupport@ yourbusinessdomain.com or sales@yourbusinessdomain.com. If your business has clients in multiple states or countries, include those territories on your Web site, business cards, and sales materials. But be smart about "office locations." Don't let this tactic backfire by saying that your company operates in New York, New Jersey, and Iraq unless you can really back it up.

Even your company's name can help you appear larger than you are. John Doe Realty sounds like a mom and pop operation. The Doe Realty Group sounds like a bigger player.

Playing your hand close to the vest is important; however, be sure that you don't leave evidence of poor workmanship to damage, undo, or tarnish your reputation. Protect and preserve your identity and image at all costs. Be careful about what you put out into the world, especially the information you upload to social networks. The last thing you want to do is have a true believer in your reputable and reliable business see old college photos of you riding a goat naked with a bottle of vodka in hand.

Never offer more information about anything than absolutely necessary. Don't give away your tactics or your secret sauce under any circumstance. How you carry yourself will determine if customers believe your company is an ant or a titan of industry. Let prospects formulate their own opinions about the size of your operation. Never lie outright to consumers, but don't feel the need to correct their perceptions either. Play to their egos, not your own, and you'll be cashing bigger checks as a result.

Analyze the advice. If someone told you to jump off the Brooklyn Bridge, would you do it? I expect not. The same applies when it comes to listening to random pundits, bloggers, and "experts" just because they are "successful"—and, yes, that includes me.

I have no illusions that every tip in this book will be an exact fit for your business needs. I'm fairly sure that most will work, a few won't, and many will help you to inform your own ideas you'll use to build your business. Start-up tips and tricks found in magazines, blogs, and TV programs are not one size fits all. What benefits one business can destroy another. There may be a considerable amount of great advice available, but it's on you to determine whether it will help *your* business to make or save real money. If not, don't waste your time.

DESIGN YOUR ENTREPRENEURIAL LIFE

Don't fool yourself into thinking that you have nothing to do and thereby rationalize taking long lunches, surfing Facebook for hours, or sleeping in—because there is *always* something to do! Thinking anything else is simply careless, irresponsible, and shortsighted.

There should never be a moment when sitting back, kicking your feet up, and taking an undeserved break seems like a viable option. Impromptu breaks and excessive inactivity will lead to nothing more than procrastination, lethargy, and insolvency. The only time it's okay to relax is when you schedule time to do so.

That's why it is essential that you consistently live according to an entrepreneurial strategy—a code of your own design that will keep you sharp, get the most out of each day, and make certain that you don't fall into a trap of unproductivity. Properly planning out how you allocate your time will reinforce your resolve, strengthen your work ethic, and increase your efficiency.

In time, your entrepreneurial strategy will become second nature—and you'll wonder how you ever lived any other way.

Make time for you. Working more hours doesn't necessarily make you more productive. In fact, toiling 24/7 to the point

---

Schedule Your Own Power Routine

Entrepreneurs who lack purpose often find themselves unfocused and disoriented. More freedom might mean you have more flexibility, but it doesn't mean that you don't need a routine. You don't need to work Monday through Friday 9 AM to 6 PM to be successful. However, just because entrepreneurship offers you a greater sense of freedom than a "real" job doesn't mean that you don't need any sort of schedule at all. You need to sketch out a power routine for producing results. Here are four tips.

1. **Determine the best work schedule**. Do this by working all seven days of the week for one month. Write down the dates and times where you had the greatest levels of success.
2. **Divide your successes into three categories: strategic planning, internal operations, and revenue generation**. Strategic planning includes activities like working on your One-Paragraph Start-Up Plan and researching local competitors. Internal operations include vendor negotiations and marketing materials creation. Revenue generation includes client meetings and cold calling prospects.

(continued)

(*continued*)

3. **Analyze your schedule's successes and failures.** What days of the week and times of the day were you most productive for each category—and why? What were the reasons your business was less productive on certain days and times? Is there a way to improve your productivity in each category by making adjustments to your daily and weekly schedules? For example, you may find that Mondays are generally quiet while Sundays are your best sales days. Perhaps your sweet spot for revenue generation is 9 AM to 2 PM Monday through Friday, and your most productive strategic planning efforts take place on Saturdays and Sundays between 8 PM to 12 AM. You may also find that certain activities would be best accomplished on the same day and time every week. Adjust your power routine until you believe it's exactly on point.

4. **Set a schedule and stick to the script.** Whatever schedule you create—whether you work Saturday to Wednesday from 3 AM to 1 PM or work seven half-days a week—be certain that your power routine is one that generates the most positive and effective results in each category. Your schedule shouldn't revolve around your nights out with friends or beautiful beach days. Work the hours of the day and the days of the week that are most conducive to your business activities. Remember, this exercise isn't meant to grant you unwarranted vacation days.

of exhaustion will result in burnout, stress, and possibly spikes in your blood pressure. It's essential to set aside personal time and learn to treasure your free time as a reward you've earned rather than something that's readily available.

Making time for fitness is also important. I promise that you will be much more productive if you take better care of yourself. If you can't afford a gym membership or to purchase equipment, create simple workout routines that you can do in your bedroom.

Do yourself a favor: Don't make excuses.

You always have time to take care of yourself. I used to be the laziest person in the world when it came to exercise— something I paid for with a lack of productivity caused by spells of exhaustion and fatigue. Stay physically and mentally strong so you can put in the time your start-up requires. Eat right, get sufficient rest, and exercise regularly.

Before you plan a single personal activity, put the proper safeguards and protocols in place to protect your business. Be sure that your standard or amended hours of operation are easily available to inquiring customers. Keep clients notified of changes to your schedule. Always be sure to offer convenient rescheduling options to clients, should you need to cancel on them. Consider implementing an emergency contact plan in case customers need immediate attention.

Then, once you've established your safeguards, unplug completely. The world will not crumble if you turn off your phone or take a short break from e-mail and texts—so long as you've taken the proper precautions and notified the right people. Make time for friends, family, personal hobbies, and activities. Only check in on your business during short, timed intervals. You'll become a happier, more effective, well-rounded business owner when you give yourself time to enjoy your life.

Create a "boredom backup plan." As I mentioned earlier in the chapter, there is *always* something to do. Fight back unproductiveness by having a boredom backup plan: A series of action items you have stored in your back pocket that are ready to be executed anytime you're about to opt to watch mindless television shows or play video games on your couch. Having this plan in place will help you stay on top of your game during slow periods.

Adjust your backup plan regularly and strive to improve productivity. Remove outdated activities or any that don't generate positive results for your business. Make sure that any new tasks you add are always productive. Some people may need to spend time doing product R&D; others may need to develop new products. Don't let downtime become "you" time; otherwise you'll find yourself with much more time than you ever wanted.

Twelve Productivity Boosters to Help Save You Time and to Help Get You Organized

1. **RescueTime.com** enables you to focus your Internet usage and boost productivity by automatically tracking and analyzing your time. This site provides analytic and reporting tools and also lets you temporarily block your usage of distracting Web sites, thereby keeping your attention where it needs to be: on generating revenue! Cost: Free to $9 per month.
2. **Evernote.com** is the equivalent of digital Post-its on steroids. No matter if you're using a smart phone or your computer, you can save all of your notes, ideas, videos, photos, and Web bookmarks in one place. Cost: Free to $5 per month.
3. **Shoeboxed.com** takes all of your business cards, receipts, and other important documents, organizes your data, and stores everything in an online database. Send these documents via e-mail, snail mail, or from your mobile device. The data can be exported to a number of different address book applications and tax preparation services. Cost: Free to $49.95 per month.
4. **Box.net** is a Web-based storage service that offers a secure online storage space to share, access, and manage all of their files and content. Cost: Free to $29.95 per month.

5. **Setster.com** makes appointment-setting easy. The company's widget embeds on your Web site, enabling customers to book and prepay for appointments online 24/7—without your needing to be involved in the process. Cost: Free to $29.95 per month.

6. **Proposable.com** lets you create rich media proposals online. Its most notable feature is the ability to see when leads open your documents, as well as the specific sections they are reading in real time. Cost: Free trial to $29 per month.

7. **FreshBooks.com** lets you create quick and easy professionally branded invoices. It also provides effective bookkeeping and reporting tools that make tax season easier to manage. Cost: Free to $29.95 per month.

8. **RightSignature.com** speeds up the document-signing process by offering your clients and vendors the ability to sign contracts online. Cost: Free trial to $49 per month.

9. **BasecampHQ.com** is a project-management tool that lets you oversee multiple projects with ease by utilizing file sharing and centralizing feedback online. Cost: Free to $49 per month.

10. **Docstoc.com** is an online marketplace with templates for every kind of document you will ever need—from legal contracts to business forms to presentations. Cost: Varies.

11. **Google Apps** includes Gmail for business, Google Docs, Google Calendar, and other productivity applications that can be accessed no matter what Internet-connected device you're using. Cost: Free to $50 per user per year.

12. **Plum Choice** (www.PlumChoice.com) can handle your technical issues—whether you have a Mac or PC—in a fast and expedient manner by tapping into your computer remotely and troubleshooting your issues until they are resolved. Cost: Varies.

Get organized. There will always be plenty to worry about—hunting for a ringing telephone that's hidden under a mountain of paperwork or searching multiple devices and hard drives to locate files shouldn't be on the list. Don't drown in clutter. Keep all of your tasks written down in one easy-to-access place, preferably online, where it can be synced across all of your devices. Develop an uncomplicated organizational system. Structure your contact databases for maximum effectiveness, create searchable file systems on your computer or mobile device, and design an efficient labeling system.

Have an idea notebook with you at all times. Ideas will hit you out of the blue all the time. Unless you're prepared to jot them down at the moment of their conception, you'll forget them entirely. Your brain will be pulled in a thousand directions, and there is only so much you can possibly recall. Don't fool yourself into thinking that your extraordinary photographic memory will store every thought. No matter how foolish, crazy-sounding, or just plain useless something may seem—write it down. You never know when one of your ideas will be the catalyst that positively transforms your business.

What time is it? Ever have a moment where you looked at your watch and asked yourself, "Where did the day go?" or "Is it 5 PM already?" As an entrepreneur, it is essential to manage

---

Three Steps to Bite-Size Your Tasks and Objectives

Failing to simplify complex tasks will lead to expensive mistakes, drawn out timelines, and scattered efforts. Breaking down multipart undertakings into a series of bite-size steps will keep you motivated and allow you to accomplish goals more easily. Distilling tasks to basic elements can also help to determine the best courses of action. This trains you to simplify big projects into smaller action steps and to avoid taking on more than you can handle.

1. **Determine whether the task is simple or complex.** Simple tasks are those that contain no moving parts and can be completed in one step—like depositing funds in your bank account or responding to e-mail. Complex tasks are made up of many components and cannot be completed without achieving multiple milestones. An example of this would be building a Web site.

2. **Map out action steps.** Break out each of the components into individual items. Consider possible alternatives for each action step before settling on it. In the case of building a Web site, you might go about making the process bite-size like this:

   - Research and list available Web site development options.
   - Establish timelines and price each of these options with multiple vendors and online services.
   - Determine each available option's potential "rock bottoms."
   - Decide on the appropriate course of action.
   - Renegotiate terms to your liking with selected vendor (if applicable).
   - Hire the vendor or pay for the selected service and execute.

3. **Analyze your process based on successes and failures.** Was there a task you were unable to complete in the time frame you established? Could you have simplified any of your action steps further? What did you learn from the achieved outcomes that will help you to improve your method of dissecting tasks in the future? Asking yourself these types of questions will better prepare you to take on your next round of "to-dos" and bite-size complex task lists in the future.

your time effectively. However, proper time management is only effective if you master proper time *allocation.*

Before you perform any task or entertain any time commitment, determine first whether the activity is time-efficient or a time drain by asking yourself these four questions:

1. Is the activity *essential*?
2. Is the *timing right* or would you be better served doing something else?
3. Is your *presence absolutely necessary* to complete the task?
4. Is there a *better way* to engage in this activity?

Should you decide to take on the task, do everything in your power to remain on schedule. After completing it, assess your results with these four follow-up questions:

1. Did the activity turn out to be the *best use* of your time?
2. Was *adequate time* allotted for the activity?
3. How could your time been spent *more efficiently*?
4. Will you participate in this activity *again*? If so, under *what conditions*?

Assess your time usage daily. If you find that an activity doesn't pass muster, amend or eliminate it entirely.

"MIND" YOUR BUSINESS

Well-rounded entrepreneurs are capable of making informed decisions and thinking on their feet. It's imperative you learn *how* to think for yourself—not simply listen to others' opinions of *what* you should think.

The most important thing you can do is to learn from your mistakes—and never make the same mistake twice. Once you figure out how to nudge your way out from between a rock and a hard place on your own, ask yourself why you ended up there in the first place—and you'll be less likely to end up trapped again.

Do one thing perfectly, not 10 things poorly. Too much multitasking will result in spreading yourself too thin—which will, in turn, eat up valuable time and limit both your effectiveness and productivity. Don't feel compelled to jump at every opportunity. Just because someone offers you the chance to become an equity partner in their cool-sounding, penniless start-up or a shot to sell their untested, no-market share product alongside yours doesn't mean you should agree. You shouldn't even listen to them—because these so-called opportunities are often nothing more than distractions.

Maintain strong self-discipline to avoid getting sidetracked. Should you find your mind wandering or your actions scattered, stop and ask yourself these four questions:

1. How did you get here?
2. What caused you to lose focus?
3. What could you have done differently to tune out the distraction?
4. How can you avoid recurring distractions?

If you continuously find yourself getting easily distracted or jumping into other projects, you may be subconsciously trying to tell yourself something about your original concept.

"I can't" and "No" are lazy answers. Never accept "that's just the way it is," "that's the way you have to do it," or "that's the only way it can be done," as acceptable answers to *anything*. And don't waste your time with anyone that believes these are real answers. Unlike the corporate world, wherein your every move is predefined by a script, entrepreneurs need only keep two core principles in mind: survival and ingenuity.

Whenever you face resistance of any kind, consider each of these three options to determine the best course of action:

1. Can you go *through* it by attacking the problem head on?
2. Can you go *over or under* it by taking a different path to get a similar outcome?
3. Can you go *around* it by avoiding the obstacle entirely, and using a new approach?

You must operate in the world as it is meant to exist to you: without boundaries or borders. Don't just spew clichés such as, "I think outside of the box"—execute and make things happen. Do anything except business as usual and never let anyone or anything stand in your way. Rid your mind of preconceived barriers, and know that every problem can be solved and every obstacle can be conquered with a little thought and good sense.

Nine Resources for Young Entrepreneurs

It's essential while developing your company to keep your ear to the grindstone and stay up-to-date on the latest bootstrapping, sales, marketing, and operations strategies. Here are my top picks to keep your business a well-oiled machine.

1. *Entrepreneur* magazine and *Inc.* magazine: Offer tips, tricks, and advice from hundreds of entrepreneurs as well as stories about entrepreneurship and small business.
2. StartupNation.com: A Web site for entrepreneurs *by* entrepreneurs that provides readers with practical advice and insights for building a business.

3. **SmallBizTrends.com:** A daily blog for entrepreneurs and small business owners that features insights of many successful entrepreneurs on a wide variety of business topics.
4. **ToiletPaperEntrepreneur.com:** The blog of business how-to expert Michael Michalowicz.
5. **How to Change the World** (blog.guykawaski.com): The blog of entrepreneur guru and author Guy Kawasaki.
6. **GaryVaynerchuk.com:** The blog of social media expert and serial entrepreneur Gary Vaynerchuk.
7. **Mixergy.com:** A Web show hosted by Andrew Warner that features interviews with successful entrepreneurs in all fields and industries.
8. **TheRiseToTheTop.com:** A web show hosted by mediapreneur and author David Siteman Garland that features entrepreneur interviews and business tips.
9. **OPENForum.com:** A knowledge base and resource center for small businesses and entrepreneurs sponsored by American Express.

It's *never* good enough. As a start-up, you must always strive to get the most out of each component of your business, especially when it comes to your revenue-generation efforts.

I once consulted for a local fast-food restaurant that used a branded costumed character to hand out promotional flyers outside of its location. While the owners seemed thrilled with the character's results, I was hardly impressed. After adding up the total campaign cost of the costume, flyers, and hourly manpower, I concluded that these "results" were actually bringing a loss to the business. Though the gimmick was garnering attention, it wasn't driving traffic into the store to generate immediate revenue.

To remedy the situation, we added a few interactive components to the marketing tactic. Rather than simply handing out flyers, we put a sign around the character's neck that said, "Text my pic to your friend and get free fries!" Each time someone snapped a photo of the character from their mobile device and texted it to a buddy, they received a coupon for free fries with the purchase of a large soft drink. This seemingly small modification produced substantial results.

We found that the average person who redeemed the coupon did so within a few minutes of receiving the voucher—not to mention the fact that they typically ended up buying more than large fries. We doubled the mascot's lead generation potential and built buzz organically by banking on the randomness of the text message with the character's photo to fuel conversations.

Always get the most out of every component of your business. Review each aspect of your company to determine how you can get better results.

Ask yourself "why." Ever have a little kid "why" you to death?

"It's hot out today."

"Why?"

"Because it's 101 degrees."

"Why?"

"Because there isn't a cloud in the sky, we're standing on asphalt, and the sun is out!"

"Why?"

This game can go on for hours, or until you finally can't take it anymore and just cover the kid's mouth. However, although the "why game" can be a mind-numbing and irritating activity, it can also be the difference between making a good decision and a bad decision. Ask yourself *why* you plan to engage in an activity or why something went wrong until you no longer have the ability to do so.

"Why am I behind schedule on a project?"

"Because my freelance Web designer quit mid-project."

"Why did my freelance Web designer quit?"

"Because he said the project management was in total disarray."

"Why was the project management in total disarray?"

"Because I never told my client the proper ways to send me feedback—and everything is scattered and unprioritized."

Answer to the why exercise: "Next time, I need to properly communicate how the feedback and change order process will work with my clients before the start of the project."

Think backward to move forward. Asking yourself "why" will help you better formulate hypotheses for your One-Paragraph Start-Up Plan, tighten up your Guess and Checklists, strengthen your ability to forecast a decision's rock bottom, and get to the real root causes of problems facing your business.

Surprise, you're on my team! Whether you realize it or not, every part of your surroundings was created with a purpose for a specific reason supported by a calculated series of thoughts, actions, ideas, and decisions. Learning how to interpret your environment and decode these hidden messages will lead you to build a smarter, better-informed, more strategic start-up.

Everything is done by design. There is a reason certain things are on a store's top shelf while others are on the bottom; a reason a company chooses one color palette over another for their packaging; and millions of other reasons that lead to countless other decisions. The question is—what decisions will lead others to the outcomes you're seeking?

You'd be surprised by the sheer volumes of people you have access to who can help you figure it out. Even though you don't realize it yet, you actually have access to the minds and insights of thousands of multimillion-dollar marketing gurus, top creative thinkers, and brilliant operational tacticians. And, the best part is, you don't need to pay them! In fact, they don't even know they're working for you—granted, neither did you until a few seconds ago.

In all likelihood, there are tens of thousands of similar companies and entrepreneurial minds who have traveled your path before and you have the ability to examine their actions, decisions, and outcomes to find many answers to your questions. How did a similar company go about winning market share? How can you follow similar logic to garner comparable results on a smaller scale? What led a company that targets the same demographic to develop their branding? What decisions and economic factors led a competitor to bankruptcy?

Your "team" spent lots of time and money doing research and testing the market to give you access to the information. Now use this material to your advantage. Utilize top-dog brainpower to help you formulate your daily action steps. You've bought into them long enough; it's time for them to return the favor.

Twenty-Five Mentors You Should Be Following on Twitter

Social media has made it easier than ever before to find mentors who can truly help you out and guide you along your entrepreneurial journey. Seeking out insights from like-minded individuals is now as simple as conducting a Twitter or Facebook search and pressing "like" or "follow." To get you started on building your own team of thought leaders, here is a list of 25 of mine:

1. Guy Kawasaki (@guykawasaki): Founder of AllTop.com and Garage Technology Ventures, entrepreneurship guru

and best-selling author of numerous best sellers, including *The Art of the Start.*

2. Anita Campbell (@smallbiztrends): Founder and editor in chief of SmallBizTrends.com.

3. Robert Kiyosaki (@rich_dad): Personal finance guru, blogger, and author of numerous best-selling books, including *Rich Dad Poor Dad.*

4. Gary Vaynerchuk (@garyvee): Social media guru, the host of WineLibraryTV.com, and author of *Crush It!*

5. Amy Cosper (@EntMagazineAmy): Editor in chief of *Entrepreneur* magazine.

6. Chris Brogan (@chrisbrogan): Online marketing expert, president of New Marketing Labs, and author of the best seller *Trust Agents.*

7. Tony Hsieh (@zappos): Customer service expert, author of *Delivering Happiness,* and the founder of Zappos.com.

8. John Jantsch (@ducttape): Marketing blogger, author of *Duct Tape Marketing* and creator of a systematic small business marketing system by the same name.

9. Sarah Evans (@prsarahevans): Public relations and new media expert, and author of the PRsarahevans.com blog.

10. Mike Michalowicz (@TPEntrepreneur): Serial entrepreneur and author of *The Toilet Paper Entrepreneur.*

11. Tim Ferriss (@tferriss): Productivity guru and author of the best-selling book *The Four-Hour Workweek.*

12. Andrew Warner (@AndrewWarner): Serial entrepreneur and founder of Mixergy.com.

13. Henry Blodget (@hblodget): Editor in chief of the *Business Insider* (BusinessInsider.com).

14. Adam Toren (@thebizguy): Serial entrepreneur and cofounder of YoungEntrepreneur.com.

(continued)

(*continued*)

15. Donna Fenn (@donnafenn): Small business and entrepreneur journalist, *Inc.* magazine columnist, in author of *Upstarts!*

16. Adam Ostrow (@Adamostrow): Editor in chief of Mashable.com.

17. Brian Clark (@copyblogger): Copywriting and online content expert, and founder of CopyBlogger.com.

18. Aaron Wall (@aaronwall): Search engine optimization expert, and founder of SEOBook.com.

19. Matt Wilson (@MattWilsontv): Serial young entrepreneur and founder of the Under30CEO.com blog.

20. Shama Kabani (@shama): Social media marketing expert and author of *The Zen of Social Media Marketing.*

21. Chris Guillebeau (@chrisguillebeau): Author of *The Art of Non-Conformity* book and blog (www.chrisguillebeau.com).

22. Darren Rowse (@problogger): Blogging expert and founder of ProBlogger.net.

23. Dan Schawbel (@danschawbel): Personal branding guru and founder of PersonalBrandingBlog.com and *Personal Branding* magazine.

24. Pamela Slim (@pamslim): Business coach, writer, and author of the book *Escape from Cubicle Nation.*

25. Richard Branson (@richardbranson): Founder of Virgin.

8

SHOESTRAPPING (BECAUSE THE BOOT IS TOO DAMN EXPENSIVE)

A few weeks after shutting down *the company that shalt not be named*, I felt obligated to review the line items on the credit card statements that I was so resentfully paying off. Never before in my life had I felt compelled to punch a hole in a wall—but I guess there's a first time for everything. It didn't take more than a few seconds to figure out that poor cash-flow management was a major reason the company went kaput.

Come to think of it, "management" probably isn't the right word. "Reckless mismanagement to the point of decimation" is actually more like it.

Our start-up philosophy was hardly one of meticulous bootstrapping or growth with client revenues. It was more of a "purchase first, and never ask questions later" approach. Before we earned a single cent in revenue, we were already in the hole for thousands of dollars. Here are a handful of the knuckle-headed, amateurish financial mistakes we made:

- Rented pricy office space prematurely.
- Hired employees before we could afford it.
- Paid high-priced consultants to tell us information we could have found online for free.
- Purchased overpriced presentation materials.
- Failed to negotiate with and often accepted the first project bid from friends.

Cash flow is the most important thing for your business. Your wallet and bank account are your company's lifeblood. Yes, it's important for your company to look like a polished and experienced brand, but it is equally—if not more—imperative to maximize existing resources, maintain a low overhead, and manage cash flow effectively. It's time for you to learn how to be a cheapskate, outsource effectively, and look like a million-dollar enterprise without bleeding red.

FAKE IT 'TIL YOU MAKE IT

Your company simply can't afford to make a poor first impression in today's cluttered, hypercompetitive marketplace. Every touch point that leads to your business needs to impress, motivate, and inspire potential customers. You may have a great product or service, but if you want to be taken seriously, you need clients to believe that you're on the same playing field as the bigger guys.

Fear not. You needn't spend millions to make it seem like you're worth millions. Your start-up needs little more than a phone number and an e-mail address in order to position itself to look and sound like a multimillion-dollar enterprise.

Look like a big fish with a $10-a-month Web site. Your Web site is the center of your brand universe—and simplicity is the key to looking like a multimillion-dollar enterprise. Don't get discouraged if you don't know how to construct a Web site. Frankly, bothering to do this from scratch is a waste of your time anyway.

Unless you're an expert Web programmer and graphics designer, building a custom Web site comes with the high-opportunity cost of wasted time. While I normally advocate that you outsource as much as possible, Web sites are a different animal. Hiring programmers from India or Ukraine might seem like a great solution at first, but $2 an hour will not make up for language barriers and a lack of any support whatsoever. Agencies and firms are cost-prohibitive for start-ups and can turn the simplest of Web projects into full-blown money pits—and a good amount of those Craigslist posters you see are just frauds out to bamboozle you.

This is why the smartest start-up Web sites are those no one has to build—and the ones that can be up and running in 20 minutes.

There are a variety of cheap, reliable subscription-based service providers that offer small businesses online tools, ecommerce stores, well-designed templates, and hosting packages that can have your site up quickly without the necessity for

---

Services that Can Help You Launch a Low-Cost Web Site Fast

There are several online services that can give you the Web presence your business needs at a price that won't break the bank. Here are my top choices for free and inexpensive services that will get you online and generating income in no time:

- **Weebly.com** provides professional templates, free hosting, domain name registrations, and a wide array of design and customization tools that allow you to easily update your site in minutes. Cost: Free to $60 per year.
- **Shopify.com** powers the ecommerce section of your Web site by enabling you to sell products online, customize your own Web stores without any design or coding knowledge, accept credit card payments, and create custom domain names. Cost: $24 to $99 per month.
- **PayPal.com** allows you to collect receivables faster by offering your clients a way to pay their bills by credit card via their mobile devices or online. Cost: Free to $30 per month plus transaction fees.
- **MoFuse.com** enables you to create a custom, search engine–friendly mobile Web site in the click of a few buttons. Cost: $7.95 to $89.95 per month.

Web development or coding experience. Most importantly, these relatively inexpensive services eliminate the need for large chunks of cash and maintenance fees up front, and enable you to update your content with a few keystrokes and couple of clicks of a mouse. There are also an abundance of available freeware technologies that make it easier than ever to add blogs, forums, video, and forms to your Web site.

The best, most professional Web sites are those that load the fastest, are easy to navigate and understand, offer the most relevant and valuable content, and successfully convert users into satisfied customers and information providers. "Best" does not mean "most complex" or "pretty."

In other words—less is more. A clean, simple-to-navigate, easy-to-read two-page site with useful content makes your company look far more established than a cluttered 20-page site with long-winded fluff. Make sure that users can find any pertinent information in no more than two clicks. Ditch the unnecessary sections—such as half-assed "About Us" pages— and place the most important content above the fold.

As your cash flow increases and your business flourishes, you can consider hiring Web design firms and programmers. But until then, forget the bells and whistles; keep it small, simple, and solely focused on revenue generation. You'll look like a captain of industry as a result.

Be the master of your domain (name). Choosing the right URL plays a vital part in your brand development strategy. Domain names can either turn users onto your site—or turn them off completely. A good one will draw users in to learn more about your company. A bad URL will have them pigeon-holing you in the blink of an eye and scrolling to the next Google search result.

Your main URL should be no more than 10 to 15 characters long. Lengthy URLs are hard to remember, hard to read, and are likely to be spelled incorrectly. Use domain names with a ".com" extension. Although it's important to purchase all of the other domain extensions to protect your name, major companies rarely use extensions such as ".tv" and ".net." Avoid using URLs that are sentences, begin with lackluster words, or utilize dashes for your main Web site. A funky URL for a landing page is one thing, but there is a reason Apple's main Web site isn't WeLoveApple.com or Apple-Computers.com.

Finally, steer clear of domains that remove or add letters from correctly spelled words. This doesn't make you sound like a smrt, hipp Web 2.0 guroo—it makes you sound illiterate, announces to the world that you're a start-up, and makes it difficult for users to find your Web site. Keep in mind that your domain name also needs to make for a simple, easy-to-type e-mail address. It's highly unlikely that anyone in their right mind will think that your company is a 10-figure winner with an e-mail address like jdoe@my-strt_up-sux.info.

Keep your domain name in mind when you name and brand your company. It's nearly impossible to acquire your exact company name as a URL, but your domain name must convey and embody your brand's message to prospective customers and users. The best URLs reinforce the company's product or service offering.

Buy a vanity phone number. How often have you seen a billboard or heard a radio spot that advertises an easily forgettable phone number? Phone numbers must be catchy, memorable, and relate to your product or service to prove effective. Online services sell custom vanity numbers for around $50. Purchasing one of these vanity numbers increases the likelihood that prospects will remember your number long enough to enter it into their mobile device. A vanity number will also increase sales call volume, build brand awareness, and increase the effectiveness of your marketing efforts.

Case in point: Sizzle It! experienced a 30 percent increase in calls the month after we replaced our generic phone number with 877-EZ-SIZZLE. Our clients told us the number was easier to share with others and reinforced the simplicity of our services.

Keep in mind because of the ever-growing number of new smart phones and other mobile devices, numbers don't always match up to their alphabetical counterparts. Be sure to decode your vanity number on your business cards, marketing materials, and online. This will prevent you from losing a segment of leads that remembered the vanity number, but got frustrated trying to use it.

Use virtual phone systems. When you combine a toll-free number with an automated phone system you can make a small business look and sound like a Fortune 500 enterprise while you operate out of multiple locations anywhere in the world. These services use professionally recorded voiceover talents to welcome and thank callers, automatically route callers to the appropriate party, and provide callers with brand messaging and information while they wait on hold.

Big companies pay tens of thousands of dollars for their phone services, but small business phone systems can be as reasonable as $50 per month. This lets small business owners receive calls in their home offices or on their mobile devices while appearing to be available in an office. It also creates the appearance of a centralized office, when partners and employees might actually be on two different sides of the country.

Work in a virtual office. Though you might be answering a call on your mobile phone from your living room, it's important that your customers believe they are calling a global headquarters with an office and a staff.

For only a few hundred dollars per year, virtual mailing addresses and offices offer small businesses high-profile mailing addresses on brand name streets in major metropolitan areas. In addition, they include mail-receiving-and-forwarding services, receptionists, and options for on-location meeting space.

For example, instead of paying high New York City rental fees, my second business saved more than $100,000 by renting a Madison Avenue mailing address for $300 per year from ManhattanVirtualOffice.com. I never stepped foot into an actual office, and was only using the address to forward mail. However, putting the Manhattan address on my Web site and marketing materials gave my company such a boost in clout that we needed to increase our rates to maintain the perception. After all, Madison Avenue companies aren't cheap hires.

The best offices for start-ups don't have a view, so avoid spending any money on your "real" office space. Take advantage of any free locations that are at your disposal, like an apartment or a relative's garage. Don't sign long-term leases. If you absolutely must have a brick-and-mortar presence, consider alternatives to traditional office rentals, such as month-to-month leasing, coworking spaces, or bartering with other businesses for space.

Create a Virtual Business on a Shoestring Budget

Forget about securing office spaces and the amenities associated with them. These cash-drains can cost you thousands—even tens of thousands—of dollars every month. Chances are you'll never need to see your client face-to-face unless you're performing your service at their location. And, if you do need to meet your clients, guess what? There are services for that, too.

Perception is power, but it doesn't have to be expensive. Here are nine of my favorite virtual business services that can help you become a big presence while actually maintaining absolutely no presence at all.

1. **Regus** (www.Regus.com) enables you to set up headquarters anywhere in the world. This company offers multiple

virtual business services including mailing address rentals, mail-forwarding services, and hourly office and conference room rentals with videoconferencing capabilities, Internet access, and administrative support. Cost: Varies.

2. **Mycroburst.com** is your virtual creative team. It's an online marketplace that provides access to hundreds of designers who can create logo designs for your company. The best part? You only pay for the winning designs. Cost: Starting at $149.

3. **oDesk.com** is your virtual support staff; an online marketplace where you can find administrative, sales and marketing, design, and multimedia support. The site also enables you to track project progress, as you pay for verified billable hours. Cost: Varies.

4. **Moo.com** provides double-sided full-color business cards, minicards, and postcards on thick card stock at a fraction of the price of traditional in-house printers. Cost: $21.99 to $61.99.

5. **iPhone** enables you to do it all: make calls, e-mail clients, scan documents, write proposals, maintain your calendar— all without ever having to sit behind a desk. It's a mobile office on steroids, in one compact package. Cost: Starting at $99 plus the cost of a wireless service contract.

6. **Grasshopper.com** is a virtual phone service for entrepreneurs that enables you to make your phone sound like that of a Fortune 500 executive. This service provides unlimited extensions, thousands of free calling minutes a month, and free custom toll-free numbers. Cost: $29 to $49 per month.

7. **eFax.com** is a complete digital fax solution for small businesses that allows users to go paperless—and avoid buying expensive fax machines. Cost: $16.95 to $19.95 per month.

(continued)

(*continued*)

8. **EmailStationery.com** enables you to create custom-designed and branded e-mail signatures that can contain hyperlinks to your Web site and social media profiles and are compatible with all major e-mail clients. Cost: Starting at $99.

9. **UrbanInterns.com** connects you with paid or unpaid interns and part-time assistants who specialize in a wide variety of different tasks. Cost: Varies.

Create a multimillion-dollar business card. Now that you have a jingle-worthy toll-free number and a prestigious street address, it's time to combine all of those elements into a single tool. The business card is a vital part of the first impression experience; it's an instant reflection of you and your company's work.

Though I'll rarely advise you to spend money on something, a cheap, uninspired business card may send the wrong message— or worse, no message at all—to a prospective customer. I'm not advocating that you go overboard or spend excessive amounts on a small number of cards; just spend some time and a little extra cash designing and printing a card that will make a lasting impression. Your business card may be the only thing you leave behind to remind a prospect of you. This impression needs to be long-lasting.

Be creative, yet tasteful. Avoid using white, standard-size business cards. Choose a thicker card stock with a high-quality finish. Make the card longer, a different shape or a bold color to stand out. These printing options will increase the price of your cards, but they will pay off tenfold in the long run. Customers want to do business with companies that demonstrate their ability to provide high-quality services, and a creative business card sends that message.

THE ONLY TEAM YOUR MONEY CAN BUY

Now that you've established your fort, it's time to raise your army. However, unlike the kings of old who possessed enough gold and rations to support massive legions, your castle is going to have to make due with a few nickels and hordes of peanut butter and jelly sandwiches.

Maybe you can't afford your very own army. However, that doesn't mean you can't lead one into battle—and win.

Hire a virtual workforce. Need someone to keep you company? Get a dog. Need someone to get things done *for* your company? Get a virtual assistant. Full-time employees are likely cost-prohibitive for your start-up, and even part-time laborers can get pricey. Who needs office furniture, payroll taxes, and a human resources department? Screw that! Save yourself the headache of managing an in-house staff in the early stages of your business. You can still have a world-class team without a single person sitting beside you in an office.

Outsourcing enables you to benefit from a skilled, scalable, and on-demand labor force without the hassle of dealing with all the incidentals that come standard with full-time hires. It also allows you to hire the right person for jobs as they become available, instead of having to teach, train, or oversee a full-time staffer to take on new responsibilities.

Delegating select responsibilities will increase your overall productivity, efficiency, and revenue generation capabilities. For as little as $3 an hour, virtual assistants can handle everything from the most remedial administrative activities such as scheduling and data entry, to more skilled tasks such as customer support and sales.

But beware: Although finding the right virtual team will make you count your blessings, hiring the wrong one will have you pulling your hair out and backtracking. Before you commit to a long-term working relationship, test it out. Start off by assigning smaller tasks to judge the assistant's work ethic, productivity to time ratio, and quality of submitted work product.

To get the most out of your virtual staff, figure out what tasks are necessary to your business, but not necessary for you to handle personally. These tasks may include data mining and researching prospective leads. Once you've determined the tasks you plan to delegate, compose a list with detailed instructions. Help virtual assistants make your life easier, not harder. Most of them work for many clients at any given moment, while others are not exactly Rhodes scholars or rocket scientists. Many of the assistants come from places as far away as India and China—so know what you're getting. Spell out each detail of every task *completely*, in no uncertain terms. Be clear about the work product or service you expect to receive, and don't leave anything to interpretation.

Be careful not to make the mistake of overdelegating and pissing money away by paying someone else to doing things you can handle yourself—like answering your phones or taking dictation. Answer your own phone! Write your own e-mail! Your assistant should be given activities that will help generate revenue, save money, or keep you organized. If a task isn't producing your desired results, replace or cut the task from your checklist. If a virtual assistant isn't working out, don't bother giving him a second chance or more time to improve. Cut him loose. There are *many* more fish in the virtual assistant sea.

Keep in mind as well that there are many virtual assistants who are useless—or worse, complete scammers. Only hire an assistant with a verifiable reputation and one who uses legitimate time-tracking enabled services. Don't just bring someone into your inner circle because his or her rates are affordable; do your homework on each potential hire to find the right virtual person for the job. If you need someone who speaks Spanish to handle customer calls, make sure that person is fluent and courteous. If you need an expert data miner, pass on hiring someone whose only proficiency is bookkeeping.

Hurray for dirt-cheap labor! It will always seem like you never have enough hands to get everything done. Imagine if there was a way to get more hands for little to no money?

Well, there is! Call the intern brigade into action.

College students are always looking to pack their résumés with any valuable internships and work experience, which makes interns easy to find and in a nearly endless supply. Even better, it's becoming more common today for interns to work virtually from home or their dorm room; you don't even have to ever see them face-to-face. There are even companies that help you hire virtual interns!

Use these resources to amass your very own cadre of worker bees. Contact college career and internship counselors at local colleges and universities to find out how you can take part in their internship programs.

An internship program can offer your company great rewards when executed properly. However, the worst thing you can do is to hire interns solely for the sake of having interns. Leaving idle minds to wander can quickly turn your business into a daycare center. Know what you want from your collegiate workforce. Much like your virtual assistant task lists, plan your internship program in detail, and make it clear to them.

Interns need to be a value-add. Don't just hire every intern seeking college credit. Each of these people will represent your start-up to the outside world, so know whom you are bringing into your business. Interview candidates no differently than if you were hiring a replacement CEO, and select the ones who are the best fit for what you need done.

Get your troops in line. Never mistreat interns, but be authoritative. Make it clear they were hired to get work done in a timely manner, not party or fraternize. Offer the interns useful, relevant experiences that give them valuable business knowledge—and benefits your bottom line.

Build a Sales Force without a Payroll

Most likely, your company will have modest beginnings as a one- or two-person operation. However, just because you don't have two nickels to rub together doesn't mean that you can't have an elite sales force at your command for free—or close to it. There are many ways to generate sales without your direct involvement. Here are eight ways to amplify your sales efforts.

1. **Split paydays to use someone else's salespeople.** If you have a great service that complements another business's service offering, ask them to sell it for you in exchange for a gross revenue share.

2. **Bribe influencers to spread the word.** If your niche market-place has a few noteworthy tastemakers, experts, or semi-celebrities, encourage them to talk about your brand. Recruit them to be part of your team by offering them the opportunity to test your service for free or offer heavily discounted services to their fans.

3. **Turn customers into brand ambassadors.** Happy customers are your best salespeople. Give them a reason to sell to their friends and colleagues by offering them something worth talking about—or an offer worth working for.

4. **Sell using social buying sites.** Services such as GroupOn.com, SocialBuy.com, and LivingSocial.com allow you to get your product or service in front of tens of thousands of potential consumers in a matter of minutes by offering their online subscribers exclusive discounted deals.

5. **Build an affiliate network.** Offer an online affiliate program that gives anyone and everyone the opportunity to sell your product or service for commission. As your online sales increase, you may also be able to significantly increase the

size of your affiliate program by becoming eligible to work with services such as Commission Junction (CJ.com).

6. **Convert online leads into customers with avatars and virtual spokespeople.** Services such as Sitepal.com and YakkingHeads.com let you create animated avatars and virtual spokespeople on your Web site to answer frequently asked questions, pitch your service, and tell people how to buy instantly.

7. **Sell products in online marketplaces.** Services such as eBay.com, Amazon.com, StoreEnvy.com, and CafePress .com allow you to create customized online stores where you can sell your products to a global audience 24/7.

8. **Keep your brand in customers' minds with "retargeting."** Web sites such as AdRoll.com offer retargeting advertising services that use customized display ads to draw previous visitors (who didn't convert into customers) back to your site.

Feed hungry lunchtime consultants. Nowadays, it seems that everyone is a guru, an expert, or a business coach. I've wasted more than my fair share of time and money on these so-called "experts." Most of the time, half the stuff I was spoon-fed was available on the Internet, a quarter was common sense, and the other quarter was impractical.

There's a better way to get information. Forget paying hundreds of dollars for advice. Find your own lunchtime consultants.

Whenever you need to learn something new, think about the types of people who have the information you need. If you need to learn how to pitch the media, find someone in public relations. Need legal advice? Seek out a lawyer. Play six degrees of Kevin Bacon to figure out to whom you're connected. Research people on social networking sites. Ask friends, colleagues, group organizers, and family for recommendations and introductions.

Compile a list and narrow it down to about 10 people. Introduce yourself via e-mail and invite them to lunch. Keep your e-mail introductions short, professional, and to the point. Be sure to include a little information about yourself; let them know who, if anyone, referred you to them, and share why you feel they can offer you valuable insight. Most importantly, don't send people a boilerplate e-mail. Personalize each one.

Before you take a lunchtime consultant out, plan exactly what you want to ask and what knowledge you are looking to acquire. Treat the meeting as if you are actually paying hundreds of dollars. Do not let the conversation drift off topic; make every minute count and let the other party do most of the talking. At the end of the meeting—good, bad, or useless—express your thanks and be considerate of any time and advice you received. Be sure to ask the person if you can stay in touch and follow up with a thank-you e-mail shortly after the meeting.

Don't just invite *every* expert to lunch. This exercise isn't meant to waste your time or turn you into a spammer. Be reasonably certain that you have a real chance of getting a reply and actually securing the meeting before you send out a single invitation. Be exclusive in your approach. Make sure the lunchtime consultants that take you up on your offer feel special, appreciated, and like they're part of your team.

Some of the best advice you'll ever receive will be over a salad and a soda. But if you don't put yourself out there, you'll never find out what people are willing to tell you for a hamburger.

Don't *just* hire someone. Ever! Full-time employees are expensive. In the early stages of your start-up, I advise staying away from them all together. However, if you find that you need to hire someone full time, it doesn't mean that you should suddenly feel the urge to be less frugal or budget-conscious.

Nor should you forget who is taking the real risk by bringing on a new mouth to feed. Consider these things before you put your John Hancock on any employment agreement:

- **Don't pay for age.** Age doesn't mean a candidate is better qualified, more experienced, or a better fit for the position. You're better off finding a young, hungry, quick-learning self-starter to work for considerably less money than older job seekers. The only time you should pay for age in the early stages of your start-up is if age comes with a top tier, crème de la crème Rolodex.
- **Hire above-market talent for below-market prices.** Hire employees with a supply-and-demand mentality. There are many more available workers than you'll ever need for the job you'll have available, so never pay top price for anyone. Don't just let someone tell you his or her salary range; *you* dictate the terms. And whatever the person's worth, make sure he or she earns it!
- **Avoid big titles with little experience.** Look behind impressive resumes for inherent flaws. Don't get gamed. Verify references before contacting them. You never know when someone is using his or her mother or best friend as a reference.
- **Test out newbies.** Don't rush to put new people on your payroll. Start all employees part time. Establish a trial period during which you'll field-test them for a while at a lower wage to see how much they're actually worth. If it doesn't work out, you can have a clean split without having to worry about paying a severance package.
- **Determine exactly what kind of "stuff" job seekers bring to the table.** It's important to realize that when you hire new employees, you're not just on the hook for their salaries and benefits. They also need "stuff"; and stuff has a way of adding up quickly. Every employee you hire will

need supplies, computers, mobile devices, and a whole slew of other costly items. When interviewing, find out what prospects own and see if their stuff can bring down your expenses.

- **Make sure they pay for themselves**. The first employees you hire must be revenue-generators. If you're going to pay more than you expected, make sure you're getting 10 times the work output they'd expect to deliver. Make them earn every dollar by instilling a no-risk, no-reward philosophy, and building incentives and bonuses into their pay structure. Don't hire full-time support and administrative staff for your start-up. Again—don't be lazy. Answer your own damn phones!

Meet one-callers. One-callers are individuals who have achieved a level of business and/or financial success that can open almost any door with a single phone call. Even if they've never met the person on the other end of the line, their name and reputation alone get the job done. In short, one-callers are living proof that *who* you know is often more important than *what* you know.

Many top professionals are willing to give their time and energy to counsel the *right* ambitious, smart young person. You just need to know how to properly and effectively approach them to prove that both you and your business are worth their time.

Don't select one-callers simply because they are rich, famous, smart, or "someone you'd like to meet"—because the people on that "dream list" are apt to never return your calls. Instead, construct a list of relevant individuals whose business acumen, track record, industry connections, personality, and credibility have the potential to open doors and take your business to the next level.

However, you can't just list the titans of your chosen industry on a pad and start contacting them for support. You won't make it past a receptionist with lines like, "It's been my dream to meet with Person X" or "I'm starting a new business that Person X needs to hear about." That voicemail or e-mail will get deleted in a New York minute. A one-caller once told me he would decide to help someone or not in less than 10 seconds— and that's only if that person could figure out how to get to him in the first place.

Only reach out to a one-caller if you have compelling answers to the following four key points and questions:

1. **Pinpoint your unique connection:** How is your start-up story similar to the one-caller in ways that would be of interest to him?
2. **Offer evidence:** What is the proof (or, at the minimum, a series of case studies) that demonstrates your business's viability?
3. **Know what it is you're looking for:** To which specific areas of your business can the one-caller's advice be effective, useful, and relevant?
4. **Know why your business is worth the time:** What are the concrete reasons as to why the one-caller would want to give his time to your venture?

Elite one-callers don't have time to waste. If you're lucky enough to gain the opportunity to speak with one of these people, you will only have one shot to win that person over. There's no room for error with your first impression—so prior to your conversation, find out absolutely *everything* there is to know about the one-caller. Say or offer something valid and valuable. Impress them without being a kiss-ass. Show respect without being a fan. Be confident, but not cocky. Relate your experiences to theirs. Demonstrate actual value, real potential, or tangible success. And be able to do all of these things in less than two minutes.

You may be rolling your eyes right now, thinking that this sounds like an impossible task, but I assure you it's not. These doors can be kicked down with the right boot. Well-articulated cold calls and seven-line e-mails can secure appointments with rock star entrepreneurs, billionaires, and Fortune 500 CEOs; hey, it worked for me. And some of these people are still my closest advisors and mentors to this day. Though one-callers might be in an elite league of their own, they still have something in common with you: They are human beings, and in many instances, they were once in the same position that you're in right now.

As long as you are smart about your tactics, act responsibly and professionally, and are truly convinced that the one-caller might actually respond, you have nothing to lose. Most one-callers will never give you the time of day—but it only takes one to change your life, and your business.

DO WHAT MAKES CENTS

Although every pundit and his or her mother will tell you to slash expenses and cut overhead, precious few will actually provide a methodology for cost cutting. Whenever I'm in need of a product or service, my first instinct is never to buy it. Instead, I use a six-step process to determine the best method of getting what I need.

1. Do I *really* need it?
2. Can I get it for free?
3. If I can't get it for free, can I borrow it from someone else?
4. If I can't borrow it, can I barter my services for it?
5. If I can't barter for it, can I partner with someone to share the expense?
6. If I can't partner on it, how can I purchase it for the best price with the best terms?

Analyzing expenses this way will make you a more fiscally responsible business owner—one who's never bowled over by their life burn rate. Train yourself to think through every purchase in this fashion. Fight the impulse to reach for your credit card every time you need something.

Live without it. Purchasing an expensive piece of equipment might move your business forward faster—but it's unacceptable to put your company into hoc as a result. Just because you "need" something doesn't mean you can go ahead and simply buy it.

Consider the following questions before deciding to pursue a purchase: Do you really *need* to make this purchase, or would you *like* to make this purchase? Is this purchase a necessity or a convenience? Is there an alternative that will allow you to be just as successful for less? Can you hold off on this purchase until a later date when you have more cash flow to support such an expense?

The best things in life are free. Creative entrepreneurs don't just look for free stuff—they also find ways to make stuff free. Think about how you could turn a potential purchase into a freebie. Can you avoid costly software by using ad-supported Web products? Do you have what it takes to master the art of the in-store return policy? Can you string together an everlasting series of trial periods?

Keep in mind that "free" can end up being expensive. *Always* read the fine print to find out the real cost—not just in terms of money. Will you be hampered by a lack of technical support or customer service? Does the product lack quality? Is it completely developed or still being beta-tested? Will you constantly be bombarded by advertisements and junk mail in exchange for the service or product? Does "free" come with time limits, future costs, or strings attached? Is the company that supports the service credible, or a fly-by-night enterprise without an address or phone number?

Promise to give it right back. Do you only need something for a limited time? If so, see if someone in your social, personal, or business network owns whatever it is that you need. Saying "pretty please" often results in saving a pretty penny.

Put the *art* in barter. Bartering is an effective way to trade services with another vendor to get your desired product or service. In many instances, it may be less expensive for your cleaning business to clean another business's office in exchange for its accounting services than it would be to purchase the services outright.

Split the bill. Whether virtual or brick-and-mortar, every business shares certain products and services; think toilet paper and coffee, for instance. Find complementary, non-competitive purchasing partners with whom you can split your expenses. These partnerships will also enable you to save money and dramatically reduce your costs by purchasing in bulk or wholesale.

Channel your inner cheapskate. If you absolutely *need* to buy something, take the time to shop around for the best deal and purchasing options. Never pay retail price if you can avoid it. Be thrifty and aim to get the most out of every buck. Consider these six steps before swiping your corporate card:

1. Look into used, refurbished, or secondhand products before purchasing new ones.
2. Shop for bargains by using shopping comparison Web sites.
3. Check for all available corporate rates, coupons, and discounts.
4. Compare financing options from different vendors.
5. Look into purchasing alternatives such as leasing and rental programs.
6. Go around middlemen and purchase goods directly from manufacturers.

CASH FLOW OR DIE!

Plain and simple: Without cash flow you're dead in the water. And you need to be able to defend your cash flow with everything you've got in order to stay afloat. Put the right protocols and systems in place to minimize overhead during your business's infancy to keep it lean and mean in adulthood.

Enter the market yesterday. Your clients and customers are your best investors and R&D team. Limit planning time and shorten development cycles to get into the market faster. The bells and whistles can come later, but your essential services need to be validated by the market and generate revenue as soon as possible. Sizzle It! started producing sizzle reels months before we invested in our Web site. Selling what we had allowed us to improve our service to the level that we wanted with cash flow, thereby offering new clients even more reasons to hire us, and old clients more reasons to tell others about us.

Grow and fund your start-up with customer revenues. Fix and improve upon your service as you go. It's always better to improve your product offering based on what your clients actually need, not based on what you *think* your clients need.

Get piggyback rides. Piggybacking on the infrastructure of an established company can offer your start-up access to shared office space, resources, new client prospects and personnel. These strategic partnerships are based on barter deals or revenue sharing and are meant to combine both parties' resources to make the collective stronger and more productive. In short: Determine who the right partners are—the ones who can make more money with you and for you.

Identify bigger players who are good strategic partners for your company, and figure out ways to pitch them about your start-up's value. Consider the answers to these three questions while you craft your strategic partner pitch:

1. Will your product help them lower their cost to produce goods? If so, how?
2. Is your service a great add-on to their existing offerings? If so, what are the reasons why it's a natural fit?

3. Will bringing your product or service in-house give your potential partner a competitive edge, offer them access to a strategic growth opportunity, or win them more clients? If so, how?

Whatever the case may be, reach out to compatible, like-minded companies to develop win-win strategic partnerships that keep revenues high and overhead low.

Reduce, reuse, and recycle. Before you label something as junk, see if it still has some mileage in it or if it has the ability to teach you how to be more efficient in the future. Ask yourself these three questions before you throw anything in the trash:

1. Can you reduce the need to purchase or use a similar item in the future?
2. Can you save money by reusing this item?
3. Can you use the item to avoid another purchase?

Little changes can make a big impact. Switching from bottled water to tap water can save you hundreds of dollars a year. Refilling old printer cartridges can bring new life to an existing asset. Old business cards can be reborn as note cards. Don't be so quick to throw things out. Analyze your junk before it hits the landfill. Even garbage has a way of telling you how to run a leaner business.

Don't be a bank. It's hard enough to collect your revenue in a reasonable time period. Don't give clients more reasons to string you along. Establish procedures to collect accounts receivable as quickly as possible. Have clients sign contracts that clearly stipulate your fee collection schedule, preferred method of payment, and the terms for penalties and late fees.

Get a down payment before a job begins. Typically, companies will either collect 50 percent down and 50 percent on completion, or 50 percent down, 25 percent based on a midway milestone and 25 percent on completion. Figure out your hard costs and determine what payment schedule is best for you. Also discern what forms of payment—such as check, cash, and credit cards—are most likely to get you paid faster.

Keep better credit and early payment incentives in your back pocket only to be used as a reward for repeat customers. *Never* offer credit to first-time customers. Make them earn convenience and good faith. Your business will feel a big difference between cash on delivery and cash within 45 to 60 days—or even 90 to 120 days.

Zero percent interest is your best friend. The right credit card can make the difference between cash flow and cash crunch. Used correctly and maturely, a credit card will enable you to maintain a positive cash flow, stick to a budget, and easily track your expenditures for bookkeeping and taxes.

Compare credit cards from various companies to see which one is the best fit for you. Talk to customer representatives to get a sense for their level of support. Ideally, you want to sign up for fee-free cards with low interest rates or zero percent interest offers whose incentive offers and rewards programs are most conducive to your business needs.

Once you select a credit card, charge *every business purchase*. Never pay for anything in cash. I don't care if you buy a stick of chewing gum—if it's for your company, charge it to create a record of the purchase in a secure location that can be called on if need be at a later date. More importantly, avoid carrying a balance unless you have a zero percent interest card. And even if you do get a zero percent interest card, be sure to pay off the outstanding balances as regularly as possible so you don't get tripped up later with ballooned interest payments.

Avoid spending hours upon hours looking for long lost receipts on April 14 at midnight. Trust me—you'll be thanking me when the taxman comes. Don't miss out on potential refunds. Business write-offs are as good as cash in your pocket.

Eight Services to Sell Clients without Leaving Home

Travel and meeting expenses can quickly add up and burn a hole in your pocket. That's why it's best to minimize the need for airline, car travel, and hotel fees whenever possible. However, that doesn't mean you should limit your marketplace; it just means that you need to sell your product or service by using more cost-effective tools.

Keep costs down with virtual meetings, video conferencing, and online presentations. Here are my eight favorite travel-eliminating presentation tools:

1. **SlideRocket.com** allows you to create dynamic, themed slide presentations online through your browser. The presentations can include Flash, videos, photos, graphics, and music. The site also measures the effectiveness of each slide in your presentation. Cost: Free to $24 per month.
2. **SlideShare.net** allows you to share slide presentations publicly or privately on Web sites, blogs, and social networks. Cost: Free.
3. **Screenr.com** enables Web-based video production to demonstrate your product or service via Twitter, mobile devices, and over the Web. Cost: Free.
4. **Meebo.com** is a free program that aggregates your instant-messaging profiles, to enable chatting with clients and coworkers on any social network or IM tool. Cost: Free.
5. **Animoto.com** enables you to instantly create fun, hip videos out of your existing media. The service also allows you to embed marketing messages and hyperlinks to your Web site into the videos. Cost: Free to $249 per year.
6. **DimDim.com** allows you to host live meetings and webinars through your browser as well as share files,

> presentations, Web pages, and whiteboards. Cost: Free to
> $69 per month.
> 7. **FreeConferenceCall.com** provides you a free number for
>   dial-in access to a private conference-call line 24/7. You can
>   host an unlimited number of six-hour phone calls with up
>   to 96 participants. Cost: Free to varies.
> 8. **Skype** enables users to connect with anyone in the world
>   via instant message, file sharing, and free video and voice
>   calling. Cost: Free to varies.

Go paperless. There is no better way to complement your
virtual office than filling it with virtual supplies. Creating a
digital and mobile work environment can eliminate most of
your office-supply expenses. By establishing a digital workflow,
Sizzle It! was able to cut down its office supply usage by more
than 90 percent and save the company an estimated $10,000
per year.

Eliminate the need for filing cabinets and bulky file folders.
Store and automatically back up your documents on hard
drives or virtually with cloud storage. Save paper and post-
age by communicating with clients and suppliers via e-mail
instead of mailings and by reading messages and documents
off your computer screen instead of printing them. Skip the
fax machine; scan and e-mail documents instead. Cut down
on your need for checks and envelopes by using online bill-pay
tools. Make freemium work for your business by using Web-
based applications instead of purchasing costly software.

Every dollar saved on office expenses is one more buck you'll
have to pay yourself or spend on marketing. For the supplies
you really need to purchase, buy in bulk and choose generics
over brand names.

Vendors aren't your friends. Do your hired service providers pay your rent? No. Do they buy your clothes or feed you? No. Then don't help them make more money at your expense.

Instead, force vendors to earn your business.

Don't fall for bogus case studies and exaggerated sales talk. I assure you that no matter how jazzed the salesperson on the phone gets you about their service, your success won't achieve the same level attained by their magical case studies. Do your own diligence. Locate the vendor's past and present non–case study clients to check out the average results for yourself.

Don't be a jerk merely for the sake of being a jerk—but don't let yourself get bullied around, either. Negotiate fiercely with a walkaway mentality. Fight for better payment plans and credit terms, and encourage them to sweeten the pot with steep discounts, additional services and introductions to potential clients. Basically, request everything you wouldn't want to do for your own clients. And never accept first-round bids for any reason.

Haggle. And then haggle some more. Pit vendors against one another by playing their bids off one another. If a vendor doesn't give you what you want and you believe you're being absolutely reasonable, walk away and find somebody else.

Never get roped into a deal you don't want to do.

Remember, a vendor's primary goal is to sell you product or service, not make your business a success. Vendors need you more than you need them because without you they don't make money. You have all of the power. In this one instance, abuse that power to the fullest to get what you want at the price you can afford.

9

THOSE PHONES WON'T RING THEMSELVES

THE 15 PRINCIPLES OF A POWER SELLER

In business, there is nothing quite as dreadful as the deafening sound of silence. And in the *company that shall not be named,* we weren't exactly getting migraines because of the noise.

In hindsight, we would have made more money had we subleased our office to a funeral home. No one would have been the wiser—and maybe, just maybe, we'd have actually been able to pay off the rent. "Why was it so quiet?" you ask. Here's why:

- We relied on our "uniqueness" to attract clients.
- We didn't establish any turnkey selling systems or tactics.
- Our lead-generation methods were highly untargeted and unspecific.
- Our infrastructure was not geared to sales, and neither myself nor any of the other partners directly oversaw this critical department.

You may know how great your offering is, but that doesn't mean that anyone else will give you a second look. Even if your product or service can truly save your customers money, help them become more efficient, or revolutionize the way they do business, you must always remember: Sales and marketing present uphill battles for start-ups. Your prospects don't know that they need your product. In fact, you'll find out quickly that most won't even want to hear about it or speak to you at all.

Change and decision making are two things that people generally don't want to face. In fact, most would rather put their heads in the sand and continue on with their "if it's not broke, don't fix it" mentality rather than try something new. In their minds, both of these things can lead them to problems or failure. And in this day and age, that could mean the chopping block for managers and employees *thankful* to have a job.

Persistence, passion, and patience are vital to any sales and marketing campaign. But without the right messages and tactics, your energy and hard work will fall on deaf ears and get lost in the shuffle. Before you produce a single flyer, pick up your phone to make a single call or send a single e-mail, you need to learn how to attract prospects, convert them into long-time customers, and stand out from the other guys. Now I'm going to teach you how to acquire quality leads, take the "cold" out of cold calls, and build a sustainable word-of-mouth buzz about your business on a shoestring budget.

COME OUT! COME OUT! WHEREVER YOU ARE!

The key to your lead generation success is to understand, identify, and capitalize on a series of niche marketplaces that you believe are being underserved. Niche marketplaces are small, specialized market segments within larger, viable commercial industries, such as green moms are to the parenting industry or people who buy designer dog clothes are to the overall pet industry. Locating the right leads from the start will make it a little bit easier for you to get blood from stones more frequently.

Find your niche and create your own marketplace. To identify the niche marketplace you wish to enter, determine all of the key information you will need to produce a detailed profile of your ideal target customer. Who lives in your marketplace? Why have they been underserved? How can you better serve them and unite them? What do they eat, read, earn, and wear? Why do they purchase what they purchase? What do they love and what do they hate? Where do they work and what positions do they hold? What groups and organizations do they belong to? Where do they hang out online and offline? Do they attend specific events, trade shows, meetings, and conferences? In short: What defines them?

Be sure not to cast too small or too large a net. Too specific of a marketplace can leave your pipeline bone dry, while too broad a net can open up the floodgates and drown you in untargeted leads. Whenever I want to find a good estimate of a market, I use the free ad tools on Facebook and LinkedIn. This allows me to see if my niche marketplace has five people or 50,000 by simply typing in a few keywords and selecting my target client parameters—without having to purchase a single ad on their networks. Compile your data and add your conclusions to your One Paragraph Start-Up Plan and Guess and Checklists.

Mine the data for digital footprints. Want to throw away time and money on extremely ineffective marketing campaigns? Send materials to general mailing addresses, e-mail generic info@ accounts and cold-call leads, and pitch whoever picks up the phone. However, if you want to significantly improve your chances for success, you must know exactly who you want to reach out to—down to the individual's name, title, and direct contact information.

How do you uncover that type of information? All it takes is a little bit of stealthy online detective work. Most prospect information is available online—that is, if you know how to find it. In some cases, locating it will be as simple as going to a Web site's contact page. In other cases, it will take some Internet digging.

For those prospects who don't appear right away, start your search by using keywords from your customer profile to hunt down your lead's digital footprint. Join relevant online groups, forums, feeds, and social networks to gain access to group administrators and leaders. Find brochures and press materials from past trade shows, conferences, and industry events.

Look for client testimonials on competitor Web sites, printed materials, and chat threads. Locate case studies and quotes on blogs and industry press outlets. See if the person maintains an account on Twitter. When I was handling Sizzle It!'s lead generation during its infancy, I would regularly visit press release distribution Web sites to acquire public relations professionals' contact information from the press release footers—since they were my target clients.

Sometimes having certain contact information can still be enough to solve the lead generation puzzle. I'm not advocating becoming a spammer, but if you're able to find a lead's name, company, and the format of said company's e-mail address or a department's phone number, I'm sure you can find *some way* to reach out to them with relevant information. For instance, I used to call a prospect's sales department and tell whoever answered the phone that the operator transferred me to the wrong extension. When they would ask me to whom I was supposed to be transferred, I'd tell them the PR department and ask them for the correct contact's name and extension. Whereas many receptionists would simply hang up on solicitors, I found that salespeople just wanted to get their phone lines cleared as quickly as possible.

Never purchase leads and contact information from vendors. Don't fall for the lies about "getting thousands of quality leads" instantly, or any other similar nonsense. In my experiences, most companies that sell leads are scammers and spammers whose lists are anything but fresh and fertile. Remember, the same leads you'd be purchasing have been purchased by many others many times over.

Don't piss away your cash on "easy" or "too good to be true" lead generation tactics. Do your own research, and formulate and execute your own lead-generation research and acquisition process. Remember, no one knows your exact niche marketplace better than you.

Find the preferred contact info on prospects. Don't just reach out and touch anyone; that person very well might not want to be touched in the first place. Use the data from your niche marketplace profile to determine the appropriate way to connect with key decision makers, enthusiasts, and influencers in each niche of your marketplace.

Figure out which tactics will offer you the greatest chance of success. If, for example, your marketplace is filled with hip, savvy tech enthusiasts, the best ways to contact them would probably be via e-mail, social networks, or text messaging. If, however, your market is packed with older folks who don't know the difference between CDs and DVDs, phone calls and mailers may be more appropriate. Determine the most convenient ways for your prospects to see, hear, and consume your message in a format and channel of *their* choosing—not yours. Are they always on the go and prefer e-mail or are they social butterflies who like to be engaged in face-to-face forums? Don't just assume that you know the best way to insert your message and services into your prospects' lives. Not all members of a niche marketplace want to be contacted the same way, either. You need to break down your niche marketplace into specific divisions and categories to ensure that you use the right key for the right door.

Take time to know, meet, and understand them on their own turf. Find out what makes them tick. Devoting a little time to knowing your target audience may show you that you can throw all of your costly marketing ideas out the window—because free options such as handing out flyers at a supermarket or networking in person might be all you need. Putting yourself in your customers' shoes will often open your eyes to just how misguided your assumptions about your market are. I once made the mistake of sending a $2,000 Sizzle It! postcard mailer to prospects because I thought that a mass e-mail would be automatically dismissed as spam. The tactic didn't produce a single lead. However, when I transferred the exact same offer to an e-mail blast, the result was a huge return on investment. Had I called several of my existing clients, I'd have known that most PR firms immediately discard solicitor materials as a point of policy and, as a result, I would have saved a ton of money.

SELL LIKE THERE'S NO TOMORROW—OR THERE WON'T BE

It's wonderful that you are the creator of your very own niche marketplace filled with thousands of prospects. Go you! Now the real challenge begins: Convert them into loyal, paying customers.

I'll let you in on a little secret: Most entrepreneurs are clueless about—or simply just suck at—selling. I've found in my travels that many small business owners fall into one of two categories: Overly aggressive with no concept of personal space, or meek as mice and can't muster a whimper. Some don't sell enough, while others fail to create systematic sales practices. Most waste too much time trying to convince naysayers to convert to yes-men.

The key to becoming a strong salesperson isn't having a great product or service. Those come, go, and change regularly. The trick is to create and perfect an effective selling system that builds consumer confidence, generates sales, and produces steady cash flow—one that is ready to handle any type of client, encounter, or circumstance. You can't master the art of the sale overnight. It will come through practice, constantly revising your sales arsenal, and learning from failures and successes.

The following 15-principle system will teach you how to become a power seller for your business.

Principle #1: Know What You're *Really* Selling

Do you know what you're really selling? I know you *think* you do, but I bet you don't. Don't feel bad; most other business owners don't have a clue what they're selling either.

If I were to ask you what a plumber sells, you'd probably answer by saying plumbing services or supplies. If I were to ask you what your local dry cleaner sells, your response might be cleaning services. However, if I asked you to tell me the reasons *why* you hired a specific plumber or dry cleaner, I doubt these answers would hold water.

Sure, it's a given that a plumber has plumbing skills—but what they are truly in the business of selling *isn't* plumbing. They're actually selling you the peace of mind that your pipes won't burst and the knowledge that you're covered even if they do. It's understood that dry cleaners wash and fold clothes and sheets; however, customers aren't paying them to wash their underwear. They're doing it because the service offers them convenience, more time for themselves, and the *feeling* of wearing a neatly pressed, clean dress shirt.

Understand this simple fact: Customers won't hire you for your services alone. Hundreds of thousands of people are plumbers and dry cleaners. You'll get hired because your service offers some benefit to them, and because you'll somehow be making their lives easier. Clients don't hire Sizzle It! because we produce video sizzle reels; there are thousands of video production companies that can edit videos. They hire us because we've simplified a once complicated production procedure and tailored it soup-to-nuts to our clients' workflow and project management needs.

Sell *benefits*, not services. Inspire confidence by identifying a client's pain points and explaining how you plug the holes. Before you spearhead a single pitch, take a step back and figure out what would make *you* buy your own product or service. This is not the moment to fool yourself into believing your own sales jargon. Simply saying that your service provides a cheap alternative to the competition or that it's an "innovative" product may sound great and all, but get real—I highly doubt you'd buy anything based on such a crappy pitch. You probably wouldn't listen to it in the first place.

Don't waste time selling the unsellable. All you'll be doing is alienating and frustrating quality leads for no gain whatsoever. If you wouldn't buy your own product, then don't expect that anyone else will. Modify your service offering until you would wholeheartedly fork over the cash in your wallet without a moment's hesitation.

Principle #2: Tell Your Customers You Have "U.S.P."

Nothing puts a bad taste in a customer's mouth more than asserting blatant falsehoods and exaggerations to be absolute truths. I once walked by a doctor's office that had a big sign outside his practice that read, "World Renowned Specialist." Suffice it to say, I wasn't exactly surprised when I Googled this supposedly prestigious individual later, and didn't find so much as a street address listed online.

Yes, you need to stand out from the pack, but in no way is it a smart idea to base your differentiation on total lies or hyperbole. If you're looking for surefire ways to never make a sale, simply proclaim your service the best or the world's greatest service and call it a day. However, if you're looking to stand out with real and substantial credentials, identify your unique selling proposition and sell *that* to prospective customers.

A unique selling proposition is something about your business that offers a strategic advantage over your competition. It's often the vehicle that provides the results and benefits we spoke about a moment ago. Differentiating your company from your competition is the key factor in attracting your niche market to your product or service.

Nine Ways to Generate Thousands of Leads for Free (or Damn Cheap)

Selling is, above all, always a numbers game. The more targeted leads you start with, the more likely you are to succeed. And there's no bigger pool of leads available than on the Internet. There are countless online resources that can connect with your niche marketplace in no time. Here is a list of my favorite no-and-low-cost lead-generating Web tools and tactics:

1. **BoardReader.com** allows you to find online forums where users are posting your brand language, commentary about your competitors, or information about your brand, effectively turning forum chatter into potential clients. Cost: Free.

2. **Twellow.com** is the equivalent of the Yellow Pages for Twitter. Search hundreds of categories to find prospects interested in your industry or living in your niche marketplace. Cost: Free.

3. **Search social networks** by typing your brand language into the search field on each of these sites to find prospects: Yahoo! Groups, MeetUp.com, Ning.com, LinkedIn.com, Facebook.com, Ryze.com, and Biznik.com. Cost: Free.

4. **Flowtown.com** lets you find out more about prospects for whom you have limited information. Simply import an e-mail address to the Web site, and it instantly tells you the name, occupation, location, gender, and links to social network profiles that are associated with it. Cost: Free to varies.

5. **Google Alerts** is a Web-based Google service that sends daily e-mails containing content from around the Web that features your selected queries, topics, and keywords. Cost: Free.

6. **SocialMention.com** is a real-time social media search engine that shows users who, what, and where their brand language, keywords, and company are being discussed in the social media world. Much like Google Alerts, it also offers a free daily e-mail alert feature. Cost: Free.

7. **Bump** enables you to exchange contact information with prospects instantly on the go. This iPhone and Android mobile application instantly shares contact information between two mobile devices when they are bumped together. Cost: Free.

8. **Gist.com** connects your inbox to the Web allowing you to aggregate and view important information about each of your contacts, such as social media statuses, blog updates, and other business-critical information, in real time. Cost: Free.

9. **Wufoo.com** is an HTML form editor that enables users to create and manage any kind of online form, such as invitations, contact forms, mailing list sign ups, and order forms, all without any coding or programming skills. Cost: Free to $29.95 per month.

Seize every opportunity to point out why your service is a better fit than your competitors' for your targeted market. A competitor may tout its "multiservice one-stop-shop" approach, but your niche marketplace prefers a specialist. Your competitor may be a low-cost leader, but your niche marketplace might appreciate high-quality craftsmanship at low prices. Find out what customers don't like about the competition and turn those downfalls and shortcomings into your advantages.

Principle #3: Pitch Prospects as If They Are Two-Year-Olds

Don't expect customers to know or understand anything about your offerings or their benefits. They won't have a clue. This is why your main role as chief salesperson *isn't* to sell your prospect your products and services; it's to educate. Taking the time to provide prospects with information and convenient educational tools—rather than simply trying to sell them products—is the most effective way to convert leads into paying customers.

First, you'll need a sales pitch that will serve as your main hook. Your pitch should answer six basic questions:

1. What results and benefits does your product or service offer?
2. How does your product or service work?
3. What is your unique selling proposition?
4. How long will your service take to complete?
5. How much does your product or service cost?
6. What general special offer are you offering?

If you've done your job up to this point, most of your sales pitch will stem from your most recent One-Paragraph Start-Up Plan. As with all of your materials, keep your pitch direct, simple, and on point. Dumb down anything that might confuse or go over prospects' heads. Spell everything out, speak in laypeople's terms, and use small words that don't require a thesaurus to be translated.

Once you perfect your sales pitch, the next step is to adapt it to multiple formats for each type of prospect your business will target within your niche marketplace. Much like figuring out the method of contact that best fits each of your leads, it is equally important to educate them using the mediums and channels they feel comfortable using:

- **Verbal sales pitch**. This will be used for phone calls, off-the-cuff elevator pitches, and face-to-face presentations. Your pitch should be no more than 30 seconds to a minute—and not because you're speeding through it at 90 mph. Verbal sales pitches must sound natural, authentic, and hit all of your major bullet points without sounding like contrived sales scripts.

- **Multimedia sales pitch.** This will be used for virtual meetings, e-mail pitches, and your Web site; it can be a PowerPoint slideshow, a Flash presentation, or a sizzle reel. Keep your presentations to less than 10 slides, and videos under 2 to 3 minutes.
- **Print sales pitch.** This can be a PDF download from your Web site or left behind after a face-to-face meeting. Longer documents will most likely get thrown out, passed over, or distract the reader from what's important with excessive detail. Keep all of your print materials on one page. Yes, one page! Anything other than that one page might as well not exist.

Help customers help you. Bolster your sales pitches with supplemental materials such as FAQ sheets, online knowledge bases, sample products, demos, and tutorial media. As you gain more insight about your niche marketplace, consider producing multiple versions of each of your sales pitch materials to hypertarget each customer category.

Ten Things You Need to Know to Deliver a Power Presentation

Nothing is worse than a long, drawn-out meeting that feels like a trip to the dentist. The last place you want to find yourself is leading a snooze fest or a presentation that has people checking their watches every other minute.

To be an effective salesperson, it's important to master your presentation skills and learn to engage your audience effectively with highly targeted information that gets results in the shortest period of time.

(continued)

(*continued*)

1. **Be prepared.** Always be ready for the people you're meeting. Never make anyone wait for you.

2. **Sell the jockey before the horse.** Every sale begins with your first impression. Demeanor matters. Be likeable, down-to-earth, and confident. Attract people with your enthusiasm, energy, and passion.

3. **Say it in 30 seconds or less.** Get to the point. Your prospects and potential partners have other things to do, so get them to say yes as quickly as possible. The more you say, the more you're giving people to consider. Make it easy for them: Say what needs to be said, and not a single word more.

4. **Fit the pitch to the person.** Create the right presentation, not "your" presentation. Do research before any pitch to customize applicable portions and ensure that you have all of the necessary and correct information as it pertains to the person sitting across the table—or on the other side of the Internet.

5. **Show, don't tell.** Whenever possible, keep your presentations interactive. Demonstrate your product or service firsthand to show off your results rather than just talk about them.

6. **Make it visual.** Don't kill people with excessive text. Keep slides or videos simple and clean. Focus on creating visually appealing presentations using photos, videos, audio, and graphics with minimal body text.

7. **The best presentations are conversations.** Talk *with* prospects; never lecture them, put forth mandates, or tout ultimatums. Engage and interact with the people in the room. Always encourage discussion and questions as you go.

8. **Speak plainly.** You're speaking to people, not robots. Don't use jargon or clichés to make your points. Eliminate terms such as these from your vocabulary: innovative or innovate,

out of the box, Web 2.0, next generation, original, and world's greatest. Use the tools on gobbledygook.grader.com to keep your pitches in check and jargon-free.

9. **Back up or shut up.** You are asking someone else to invest his or her time and money into your product or service. Show them that you deserve it by supporting your expertise with relevant experience and *real* results. Avoid hypothetical arguments or unsubstantiated claims. If you can't do or promise something, then find another way to sell your services until you can.

10. **Know what you are talking about.** Don't say things to try to look smart or claim anything that sounds too good to be true to close a sale. Less is not only more—it also keeps you out of trouble. Remember, you're accountable for every word that comes from your company. The smartest thing to do when you don't know something is to admit that you don't know—then figure it out within 24 hours and get back to the individual with an answer.

Principle #4: Go for Base Hits versus Home Runs

Without consistent and recurring revenue, your business won't be around very long. This is precisely why it's important to divide your prospects into two categories: base hits and home runs.

Base hits are smaller, bread-and-butter clients that are easiest to target, more readily accessible, and simpler to sell to with few decision makers, shorter sales cycles, and little red tape. Examples of base hits include small and midsize businesses and individual consultancies. These types of clients will not offer you margins you can retire on, but converting these prospects into bankable anchor clients is crucial, because they are responsible for providing you with the majority of your cash flow. These clients will also be your primary word-of-mouth influencers and reputation builders within your field and community.

Home runs may draw big cheers, but they are few and far between; so until you've worked all the kinks out of your business and have a steady flow of base hits under your belt, avoid them entirely. Home-run sales cycles are not conducive to your cash-flow requirements or your bottom line. If home runs don't turn you down at square one, the pitch process could take months or even years just to get an official rejection, if you get an answer at all.

Base run clients will attract other base run clients. And several base run clients will give you a better chance of attracting a home-run client.

Mind you, I'm certainly not advocating that you never swing for the fences. Once you knock one out of the park, others will follow. However, don't make home runs your first priority. Concentrate on getting on base and driving a few runs home to improve your record before you trade up for the heavy hitters. Once you've accumulated enough base hits to support your life burn rate, use your winning record to boost your confidence and win over future fans.

Principle #5: Underprice and Overdeliver

Plain and simple, your initial pricing strategy needs to attract base hits. Later on, you can worry about getting what you truly deserve, or take the time to break down your business model into 500 different pricing plans. Only one thing is important right now—immediate revenue.

Unlike larger competitors that must factor in their infrastructures and overhead expenses into their pricing models, you need only consider these three things: the acceptable price point range in your niche marketplace, your life burn rate, and the fixed costs associated with your product or service. These cost savings provide you an advantage. But being able to undercut the competition on price won't be enough. The best way to put a dagger through the heart of your competitors is to pack a one-two punch and kill them on service as well as price. After all, if you were happily doing business with a vendor, would a minor dollar difference really compel you to change service providers? Probably not.

When I consulted with high school memory product company Yearbook Innovation, we took on our conglomerate competition with a program called Save 20. The concept was simple: Slash competitor yearbook bids by a guaranteed 20 percent, eliminate late fees and penalties that plagued schools, and offer more design and customer support services than any of our other competitors could provide for free—while providing a product of equal or better quality than the competition. Save 20 allowed us to take a large percentage of local marketshare away from well-entrenched competitors. When Yearbook Innovation's competitors caught wind of the program and started lowering their prices to remain competitive, we took advantage of the situation by showing their clients how much they had been ripped off during their previous contract period. Over a five-year period, we found some schools would have saved nearly $100,000 if their vendor had given them the cheaper pricing to begin with. This won us even more clients.

Slash competitor prices to break their legs and open doors to more prospects. Eliminate any competitive disadvantages by at the *very* least matching their abilities. Then, throw more value into the mix in the form of free services or customer support to break their backs and close more deals. However, never let your freebies turn into cost centers or time drains. Use inexpensive tactics and perceived value adds to bend your competitors into submission.

There is always a way to top your competition. But simply claiming that you can offer more isn't enough. Overdeliver on your promises while still remaining profitable and proficient and you'll be winning more market share as a result.

Principle #6: Read the Lead

Power sellers are perceptive individuals who can discern a prospect's legitimacy and available funds instantly by using visual and audio clues. They use their findings to determine the best approach of attack—and whether it's even worth pouncing at all.

Right before you meet or speak with prospects, investigate them. Does your previous correspondence indicate serious and genuine interest or represent a general, blasé inquiry? Did you seek out the prospect or did they look for you? Does the customer's inquiry seem legitimate or a waste of time? What does the company's location, office attire, Web site, and management team tell you about your prospect's tolerance for vendor pricing? Does the vibe of the company's office scream frugal or carefree? Do their client rosters tell you how much revenue they generate? Do their previous vendors give you an idea of how much they are willing to pay for services rendered? Do their demeanors suggest they'll be dream clients or horrid nightmares?

Seek out clues to determine the best pitch, pricing model, and right amount of time needed to dedicate to each sales initiative. Look deeper into every asset and clue at your disposal—from e-mail responses to the prospect's background—to figure out everything you need to know to craft an educated, customized, and well-informed pitch. The more you know ahead of time, the more likely you'll be to strike a deal.

Principle #7: Shut Up and Listen to the Customer!

If your pitch materials are effective and generate interest, they will start a conversation, one that should be driven by your prospect, not you. Bragging about your business and telling your customer every boilerplate reason they so desperately need your service will do nothing more than compel them to hang up on you faster than a telemarketer.

Steer clear of lectures and bragging sessions. Instead, talk to perspective clients about their favorite thing: themselves. Ask them specific questions about their business to learn more about their needs. What are their major pain points? What qualities are they looking for in a product or service provider? What have they tried that hasn't worked in the past and why? What customer service do they expect to receive? What are their biggest hesitations about hiring you or a competitor?

Listen for key points and keep the tone light and conversational. Often, your customers will be more than willing to give you the exact information you need to make a sale. All you have to do is shut up and listen.

Principle #8: Pull Out the Good Guy Deals

No one wants to be proven wrong or get in trouble because they backed your product or service and it ended up going south. This is why most prospects will say no to you before you even get the chance to deliver your pitch. Saying no is always a safe bet. Unlike saying yes, no is uncomplicated, quick, and leaves little room for mistakes, errors, or negative consequences. This is why you need to have a few tricks up your sleeves that allow you to make offers to your prospects that they can't refuse.

I call these "Good Guy Deals."

Good Guy Deals are predetermined, unpublicized special offers that you can use in unique circumstances to close sales and get you "good guy" status with your prospects and clients. Preparing great Good Guy Deals can mean the difference between your business landing a new customer or losing one to a competitor.

Good Guys Deals are different for every business, but typically come in the form of price reductions, discounted services, or gifts. There are three kinds of Good Guy Deals: the unbeatable offer, the favor, and the friends and family plan.

The *unbeatable offer* is a one-time deal that your competition can't match or beat. It may be an unbeatable discount, such as 80 percent off, or an unbeatable package deal, such as 10 for the price of 1. Sizzle It!'s unbeatable offer was a "name your price" deal. This was an understandably risky proposition during the founding stages of the company, which is why I only offered it to major influencers who operated in my niche marketplace—such as trade organizations and gatekeepers to large mailing lists—that I truly believed would increase overall business and wouldn't lowball us too much.

These deals are often unprofitable but are meant to secure big fish, monster business referrers, and long-term clients. Don't just provide this opportunity to everyone and his or her mother; this should be a last resort. Make it clear to your prospect that you expect a long-term relationship and client referrals in return for the unbeatable offer.

The *favor deal* is another one-time offer used to help your customer get out of a tough spot, such as budget constraints, time crunches, or a bad experience with a competitor. The favor deal often entails going above and beyond your typical service offering for less money or completing a task in a shorter period of time in order to help someone out of a bind. Again subtly remind the client when you offer a Good Guy Deal that you expect them to return the favor with future purchases and referrals.

Finally, the *friends and family plan* is a permanent discount or deal given to select regular clients. This can be a great way to reward customers for their loyalty or seal the deal with a client who has benefited from an unbeatable offer.

Know the hard cost and minimum time requirements before implementing any Good Guy Deals. You should also know what your competition can and can't offer. If the competition is a large conglomerate, beat it with your highly personal service offers. If your competitors are smaller mom-and-pop shops, blow them out of the water with an influx of additional services that the competition can't afford to take on.

Good Guy Deals should not put you in a position where you end up overpromising and underdelivering—or worse, not being able to deliver at all. These deals are meant to bolster your position and win business. Avoid on-spec work or services produced under cost unless you determine it's absolutely necessary and warranted given the situation.

Be selective and learn to recognize which clients need an incentive to buy and which don't. These tactics aren't meant for everyday use. In fact, the faster you can rid yourself of the unbeatable deal altogether, the better off you'll be.

Most importantly—know when to walk away from a prospect and abandon a sale. Customers—not prospects—are always right. If a prospect is asking you to beat your already unbeatable offer, then they're too stupid to realize how one-sided your Good Guy Deal is and aren't worth another second of your time.

Principle #9: Push No-Brainer Up-Sells on Clients

Just because you need to offer more than the competition to sell prospects doesn't mean you should offer them everything.

Up-sells are sales that come at the tail end of a sales transaction. They are most successful when they are relevant or offer added value to the customer's purchase. Examples include extended customer service and support programs, complementary products to the main purchase, and package deals such as "buy five get one free." If you're a lawn care service provider, you might consider offering clients a premium mulch treatment for a reduced rate. If you own a tutoring service, you might sell useful educational materials such as textbooks and study guides.

Always look to increase your profit margin per transaction.

You've already done the hard part: convinced them to say yes. Now it's time to get them to say it again. Determine a series of uncomplicated, straightforward, reasonably priced offers that can increase your bottom line with minimum costs and make it a point to mention these up-sell opportunities right before the completion of a sales transaction.

Principle #10: Build a Spy Network

Face it: Most of your prospects won't translate into sales. Many won't even return calls or e-mail. But just because those who did give you the time of day didn't cough up the dough doesn't mean they still can't play a vital role in building your business's sales.

Believe it or not, a no can often prove more valuable than a yes.

If someone who ended up going with your competitor is willing to take five minutes out of their day to offer you honest criticism about why your company didn't cut it, then shut up and take it. Let them revel in their momentary superiority. After all, your objective is far more important than relishing in a fleeting power trip. Your aim must be to unknowingly convert these nonclients into free snitches about your competitors.

Encourage your spies to kick you when you're down. Courteously press them for information. Ask them why they chose another company over yours. What factors led to their decision? What didn't you offer, say, or do that might have altered the outcome? How did a competitor sway them? Did they decide to go in another direction? If so, why did they decide to do an about face or choose an alternate direction?

Get the inside track on your competitor's tactics and Good Guy Deals. Take insults and criticism now so that you can improve future sales initiatives and have the last laugh when you're standing over your competitors' graves.

Five Ways to Spy on Your Competition

You'll need to remain one step ahead of your competitors to stay on top of your game. Instantly knowing their every move and misstep will help you to quickly adapt your tactics and close up gaps in your offering to overtake the competition. Here are the six tools I use to keep competitors at arm's length everyday:

1. **Google Alerts** enables you to get daily e-mail alerts on your competition. The service is also great for getting immediate information about competitor marketing campaigns and press mentions. Cost: Free.
2. **Compete.com** allows you to analyze your competitor's keywords, view their consumer's online behavior, dissect search engine strategies, and identify other sites linking to their Web sites. Cost: Free to $199 per month.
3. **Copernic Tracker** (Copernic.com) is Web site tracking software that notifies you whenever your competitor's Web sites, social media profiles, or online forums have been modified. Cost: $49.95.
4. **SocialMention.com** allows you to keep your ear to the social media grindstone. Not only does this service help you find leads, it also shows you how your competitors are engaging social media audiences, and seeks out disenfranchised customers who've posted negative feedback about their experiences with your competitors. Cost: Free.
5. **QuarkBase.com** helps you to discover new competitors and provides comprehensive data about their Web sites and tools to analyze them. Cost: Free.

Principle #11: Avoid Fine-Print Thinking

Your products or services will put your business in the spotlight; your customer service practices will make or break it. In today's social media age, negative word-of-mouth travels faster than ever before. A happy customer may tell five friends to buy your product, but an unhappy customer will tell 5,000 strangers not to buy it under any circumstances. No matter how great your product or service is, if you can't deliver on your promises or properly manage customer expectations, your business will flatline.

Know this: Marketing sells products; customer service sells clients. One-off sales might offer temporary relief to cash-flow woes, but to survive the long-haul, you must put a strong customer service plan into place to build and support a loyal, reliable client base.

Ten Ways to Manage Your Online Reputation

Building a company can take years, even decades; but its destruction can take mere minutes. Warranted or not, one customer's comments or criticisms on a single forum or social network can quickly spiral into an all-out social media assault on your brand. Engaging users in their social media spaces allows you to address criticisms, alleviate concerns, handle customer service issues, or correct wrongdoings before irate customers morph into online terrorists. Use the following 10 tips on a regular basis to nip negative word-of-mouth in the bud before some moron's forum thread or wall post decimates your hard-earned reputation.

1. **Secure your brand name's social media username with KnowEm.com** before anyone has the chance to masquerade as your company. The free Web site allows you to check out

the availability of your brand name or preferred username on over 350 social networks. Cost: Free to $249.

2. **TweetBeep.com** and **Google Alerts** are great for keeping track of your brand image, company name, keywords, and service offerings on Twitter and across the Internet. Set up daily alerts for the most up-to-date information. Cost: Free to $20 per month.

3. **BoardReader.com** allows you to use your company name and keywords to keep track of forum chatter about your products or services. Cost: Free.

4. **Twitter's** search tool (**search.Twitter.com**) and **Hootsuite .com** make it easy to keep track of mentions and tweets containing your brand handle, service, or product. Cost: Free.

5. **IceRocket.com** enables you to use your company name and keywords to stay on top of social network commentary videos and blog posts referring to your business. Cost: Free.

6. **Blinkx.com** allows you to locate all of the online videos across all video-sharing sites mentioning your company name and keywords. Cost: Free.

7. **Contact negative posters** directly whenever possible to offer assistance, determine how to resolve an issue, or ask for the opportunity to right previous mistakes or wrongdoing.

8. **Encourage happy customers** to help you bury negative reviews with positive comments. Reach out to your customers and ask them to voice their opinions about your service online. Enlist them to post testimonials about their beneficial encounters with your company.

9. **Report abuse** or inappropriate content on any Web content that is overly abusive or malicious in nature to have it removed by webmasters and site owners.

10. **Contact webmasters** and site administrators to remove cache files of deleted negative comments so that they no longer appear in search engine results.

Principle #12: Don't Eliminate the Word "Customer" from Customer Service

Nothing infuriates me more than people who don't e-mail or call me back. Even worse are those select few people who answer phones or e-mail as if they are robotic answering machines.

You're not R2D2 from *Star Wars*, nor are you important enough to be hard to reach.

Customer service isn't a one-size-fits-all policy. Every client will have different needs, and you must do your best to cater to all of these requests in short order. Good customer service begins at the point of purchase. Immediately after you shake hands with your new client, educate her on the customer service communication options your company offers and make sure that she understands how she can interact within each channel.

No matter which methods your client uses to contact you, be accessible, responsive, and readily available. Never leave clients hanging. Take minutes, not days, to respond. Always let them know that help is on the way. Even if you can't offer immediate assistance, let them know that someone is listening. If they leave a voicemail, use a recorded message to inform him when he can expect to hear back from a company representative. If he sends you an e-mail, use automated responses to provide response times and links to additional troubleshooting resources.

Six Resources to Supercharge Your Customer Service

Customer service is a 24/7 job. Great customer service can win you referrals and return customers. Bad, slow, or ineffective customer service can lead to a boycott against your brand. This is why you want to be able to offer your customers a series of tools to help them answer their questions, connect with you directly in any way they'd like, or troubleshoot their issues as quickly and efficiently as possible. Here is a list of my favorite six customer service tools to keep your customers satisfied and your customer service department at the top of its game:

1. **Twitter** can be a 140-character lifeline for your customers. This micro-blogging site can offer your clients quick access to a customer service representative (aka you) and enables them to get in touch with you instantly in an emergency. Cost: Free.

2. **ZenDesk.com** offers you and your customers a complete, easy-to-use, online and mobile help desk and support site. Cost: $9 to $39 per month.

3. **GetSatisfaction.com** is a Web application that streamlines customer feedback, support questions and answers into a single platform that can be read and responded to by anyone. The support tool can be accessed using various consumer touch points from company Web sites to Twitter to Facebook Fan Pages. Cost: Free to $89 per month.

4. **Uservoice.com** enables you to turn popular customer feedback into improved customer service. This company's widget seemlessly embeds on your Web site and enables customers to submit feedback and vote on the most relevant submitted ideas. Cost: Free to $89 per month.

5. **SurveyMonkey.com** enables you to create customized Web-based surveys and offers users a wide variety of reporting tools to analyze the results. Cost: Free to $19.95 per month.

6. **PollDaddy.com** is an online poll and rating service that allows you to survey your community, see responses in real time, export analytical reports, and manage Twitter polls. Cost: Free to $200 per year.

Principle #13: Look Like a Titan, but Act Like a Local

If you feel that adding a personal touch is not part of a bigger growth strategy for your company—well, you're wrong. Personal touches will get you more out of business than anything else.

I once spent 50 minutes of a one-hour meeting talking about a client's pets and still won the bid over my cheaper competitors. Why? Because I made an effort to get to know her and understand her on a personal level.

Take a genuine interest in your clients' hobbies, preferences, and passions. Keep a running list of unique things about each of them. If one of your clients likes coffee, bring her a cup of Joe once in a while. Instead of buying the exact same holiday gifts for clients, look to give them something they'll value.

Don't hide behind a phone or e-mail address; put in face time with your regulars. Bend over backward for your best and most loyal customers. Treat them like people, not numbers. Make them feel special and appreciated. Giving genuine thought and paying attention to small details will go a long way toward building long-lasting loyalties. Do what the big guys can't do—be personal instead of cookie-cutter in your approach to customer service. Remember, your earliest base hit and home run clients are your most important ones. Without them, you have no revenue or word-of-mouth.

Principle #14: Force Clients to Sign Away Their Rights to Fight

You are solely responsible for setting your client's expectations. Failure to do so will let their minds run amuck and potentially bring your well-oiled process to a screeching halt.

After each sale, inform your clients in writing about everything they'll need to know—from your customer service to your return policy to your delivery dates to anything else that can be questioned. Clearly outline what your company is and isn't responsible for, as well as what is and isn't included in your client's purchase.

At Sizzle It!, we have our clients sign off on our Services and Assumptions Agreement prior to any work taking place. This is a document that lists everything they need to know about their sizzle reel, its exact production time line, and instances where additional fees may apply based on changes to the project's scope. Not only does this keep us efficient and keep the clients in-the-know, it also protects our company from potential disputes that may arise over lacks of clarity.

If you let them, your clients will take advantage of you. So do yourself a favor: Don't leave room for clients to get more than they paid for. Keep all of your written correspondence with your customers on file in case trouble arises. Be meticulous in your construction of your own Services and Assumptions Agreement. Mandate every client to sign a document that acknowledges they understand their purchase in no uncertain terms. Believe me, this will save you countless headaches later on when, inevitably, a client will fight with you over something that wasn't made clear to them—even though it probably was.

Principle #15: Make It Easy to Do Business with You

Just because *you* think something is easy doesn't mean it is for anyone else. You live and breathe your company every day, but your clients don't. They have their own lives, schedules, and priorities to deal with. To them, you're a mere pit stop. This is why it's important to regularly assess how easy, simple, and convenient it is to do business with your company.

Be prepared: What you find may shock you. You might discover that your ecommerce store forces customers to jump through one step too many, or that the company phone tree might confuse callers with too many generic options.

Be mindful that you are *not* your customer. It doesn't matter if you "get" something if your customers don't get it or worse—don't like it.

There is always a way to make things easier—and no one knows how to do that better than your existing clients. So give your customers a reason to criticize your business. Offer them incentives in exchange for participating in surveys. Ask them where there is room for improvements.

Most importantly, don't just sit on feedback—act on it. Show your clients that you're actually listening to them. Be sure to let them know if their insights lead to real changes in your business.

10

FACEBOOK ISN'T A MARKETING STRATEGY

Above all else, I credit the failure of *the company that shalt not be named* to one key flaw: The fact that our marketing was practically nonexistent—and what did exist quite frankly sucked. From our useless "evolution needs a spark" tagline to our lack of a cohesive campaign, we never marketed our services effectively. Here is a sampling of our marketing failures:

- Our brand message was poorly developed, generic, and impractical.
- We were reactive—not proactive—marketers.
- We focused too much on brand marketing and not enough on actually selling our services.
- Our marketing campaigns were highly untargeted and un-unified.
- We spent too much money on ineffective ad placements.
- We failed to leverage the credible clients who were already on our roster to help us secure others.

Many aspiring entrepreneurs nowadays foolishly believe that all they need to do is sign up for a Twitter account, blog about special offers, hand out a flashy looking brochure—and they're set. Leads will come pouring in with every status update. Every flyer handed out or newsletter sent will generate big results. Each mention of the company in the press will convert into revenue. And in no time, the business will become the leading service provider simply because "that's what happens."

This flawed logic couldn't be further from the truth.

These social media fantasies and free marketing delusions would have amateurs believe that thousands of loyal customers are a mere five minutes away. Yet the mere existence of a market for your product or service does not guarantee that anyone will listen or care about your brand. People are bombarded with thousands of messages every day, which makes it difficult for business owners to garner attention and convert that attention into income.

It's true that there are a million ways to let the world know about your brand these days. However, without a quality message, creativity, and supportive offers, your business will undoubtedly get lost among the glut of content already clogging the channel. To break through the clutter, you will need to produce a marketing system that effectively converts time, energy, and brand awareness into revenue—and the only way to do this is to create effective marketing messages, become an expert in your field, and build an ever-growing multichannel platform from which to sell your products and services.

MESSAGE BEFORE PLATFORM

Face it: Any idiot can launch a Facebook Fan Page, upload a video to YouTube, or tweet about a well-written magazine article until he gets carpel tunnel. Effective marketers don't base their entire campaigns on individual tools, platforms, or channels. Nor do they simply spout off discounts or promotions ad nauseam hoping for a return on their investments.

Think about it. If someone doesn't believe in your brand or care what it stands for, what makes you believe they'll give a second look to your 20-percent-off coupon?

Effective marketing is about crafting and distributing *targeted* messages through the appropriate consumer touch points to build and maintain a powerful brand identity. The key is to develop the right supportive media—relevant information, content, call-to-action messaging and complimentary offers—that work together to attract and form bonds with prospects—and compel them to make purchases and referrals as a result.

All of this begins by creating a powerful, viable brand message that establishes your market position, effectively sets the foundation for your marketing efforts, and lets customers know what you stand for.

Create a brand language. Begin building your marketing campaign by conceiving and owning a solid *brand language*—a series of keywords and phrases that capture customers' attention. This language is used to inform those consumers of what you do and—with enough attention, consistency, and effort—will one day become synonymous with your brand name—like "copy" is to Xerox, "online search" is to Google, or "sizzle reels" are to Sizzle It!'s

If you own your brand language online, your site—as well as other Web sites and media that support your Web site and its offerings—will be the first result that prospective customers see every time they type your keywords and phrases into a search engine. Start this process by identifying keywords and phrases that are highly relevant to your product or service. In the early stages of your company, your brand language should consist of no more than three or four words. Likewise, it is important to make certain your brand language is uniquely yours so you can really "own" it. For example, an environmentally friendly car-wash business may never be able to own the words "car wash" because of the sheer number of car washes in the world, but it may be able to own the phrase "eco-friendly car wash" or "Smithtown's eco-friendly car wash."

Owning a language is worthless if it doesn't create mental associations and connect customers to your product, service, or brand. It's important to check your brand language's strength for consumer relevancy by finding out how often these keywords are searched online. Entrepreneur.com offers a keyword search tool, and other sites such as Network Solutions or Google Insights can help you narrow down your verbiage. The more relevant your keywords and the more often they are searched online, the better they'll serve you for both offline and online initiatives.

Once you've selected your main keywords and phrases, you'll need to incorporate your brand language into all of your consumer touch points—from taglines to company bios to voicemail boxes to marketing materials to social media sites. This will ensure that everything your clients and prospects see, hear, or feel conveys a cohesive brand identity.

Nine Ways to Become a Google Superstar

The Web is the great equalizer in business. Billion-dollar businesses and start-ups compete on an even playing field for Internet exposure every single day. To the victor go the spoils: Top rankings on major search engines that can skyrocket a business's revenue.

The strategy of placing brand language and keywords in targeted online spaces to gain exposure is known as search engine optimization, or SEO. Mastering this practice will increase the number of links that drive traffic to your site and the amount of real estate you control on the Web—which significantly increases your site's visibility on search engines.

Here are nine ways to master the art of SEO and to get to the top spot on online searches.

1. **Register your Web site on search engines and online directories.** Google, Bing, and other search engines allow you to add your URL to their databases and help them to find your Web site for free. Since the search engines all have their own requirements, take time to locate and follow the input instructions. There are also paid services such as Web.com's Visibility Online service (Cost: $76.95 per month) that you can use to register your Web site with search engines, maintain your SEO program, and receive on-demand SEO reports detailing ways to improve your Web site's online visibility.

(continued)

(*continued*)

It's equally important to research and create company profiles on relevant online directories such as Angie's List, DMOZ.org, SearchLocal, Yelp, MerchantCircle, SuperPages, and Google Business Center. The more credible links that lead to your site, the higher your page-rank and the better your chances are that you'll appear in search results.

2. **Optimize your Web site.** Making your Web site search engine friendly is vital to improving your online visibility. For starters, you'll need a Web site header title that's no longer than 70 to 80 characters, and a site description no more than 200 characters. Both the title and the description must include all of your brand language. You'll also want to make sure that all of your keywords and phrases are included at least once in your site's meta tags, search engine description, and body text. Do not overuse them, as this may cause some search engines to define your site as spam, which will result in lower page rank.

3. **Distribute optimized press releases.** Distributing and posting press releases online monthly will create a large number of link-backs to your site—which will, in turn, increase your visibility and site ranking. When drafting your press releases, include your keywords and phrases once or—at most—twice within the body text. Once you lock your copy, embed the appropriate links back to your Web site by using your keywords and phrases as anchor text. To avoid having search engines read your releases as spam, only hyperlink one keyword or phrase per 100 characters. In some cases, press release distribution services, such as PR Web, will have you create hyperlinks by using their proprietary software. In all other cases, use w3schools.com to find out how to write an HTML hyperlink code. Use wire services such as PR Web

(Cost: Varies) and free services such as PRLog.com to distribute your release to hundreds of Web sites and social media
networks. There are also many Web sites where you can post
and share your press release for free. Visit this link to see a list
of more than 50: http://tinyurl.com/ngarjpressreleases.

4. **Create online video and social media channels.** Social
media and online video sites offer your brand the chance to
control hundreds of pages of prime real estate on the
Internet, many of which have high site rankings. Populate
all of your profiles with your company tagline, bio, and Web
site URL. Most importantly, include your brand language
and keywords in the headlines, descriptions, and tags of all
your images, videos, media files, and social media posts.

5. **Create online content to connect popular keywords to
your brand language.** Newsletters, articles, and blogs that
offer valuable content can exponentially increase a site's
exposure in search engines. If you're creating the content,
make sure that your headline and first paragraph are rich
with keywords and brand language. Link keyword-filled
phrases back to your Web site. Avoid link-dumping by
selecting a few meaningful phrases at a time. Surround
your keywords and brand language with descriptive text,
which will help search engines determine the relevancy of
your subject matter to a search query.

6. **Syndicate, share, and bookmark your media.** Each placement
of your brand name, content, and URL on the Web increases
the possibility that prospects will find it and click. Syndicate
your own articles and blogs across the Internet by using
sites such as iSnare.com (Cost: $10 to varies). Share your
online content using social-bookmarking sites, such as Digg,
Delicious, and StumbleUpon, and using auto-syndication
services such as OnlyWire.com (Cost: Free to $24.99 per year)

(*continued*)

(*continued*)

and Ping.fm (Cost: Free). Enable users to share the content easily as well by integrating free social media tools such as ShareThis and TweetMeme into your newsletters, blogs, and Web site. Social-bookmarking sites and other social media sharing tools pull the header of your content onto their sites, so be sure that you always include your brand language.

7. **Guest blog and comment regularly**. Comments and guest posts on relevant industry threads, Web sites, and forums is another way to create valuable link-backs to your site. Make a list of the top blogs and online sites in your industry by using sites such as AllTop.com and Technorati.com. You may be able to offer your services as a guest blogger, and as such, include your brand language and company credentials along with your posts. For all other sites on your list, comment and respond regularly to posts made by site content providers with relevant advice that incorporates your brand language and Web site URL. Avoid self-promotion or spam messaging. Whenever you register a user account, use one of your keywords or phrases as your username and link it to your Web site URL. In many cases, usernames become hyperlinks when your comments go live.

8. **Swap links with other Web sites and social media friends.** One of the most important parts of SEO is getting links to lead to your Web site from other high page-ranked sites. Don't be shy about this; ask customers, friends, and partners if they'd be interested in swapping links and or sharing content with their friends, fans, and followers.

9. **Stay in the know about the latest SEO tips and tricks.** The Web is constantly changing—as are the strategies and tools needed to take advantage of it. Use resource sites such as SEOmoz.org or SEOBook.com to keep your SEO arsenal up-to-date.

Say what you do, and do what you say. Sending out mixed signals, incoherent messages, or half-assed offers will only do one thing: guarantee that *no one* will care about your brand. Furthermore, if you don't make it clear who you are and what you offer, you'll be leaving yourself open to attack, potentially enabling naysayers and competitors the opportunity to control your message.

For example: "I'm a Mac and I'm a PC." Need I say more?

You must control your message with relevancy, uniformity, and delivery. But first, you must create an active brand message to establish your principles, define your brand and—most importantly—put your business on track to generate immediate revenue.

An active brand message is a one-sentence pitch that makes a promise to prospects followed by a promotion guaranteeing that promise. The efficacy of your active brand message will hinge on this one-liner, which should immediately convey what your business does and the results it can provide. The purpose is to attract customers and fuel word-of-mouth. You'll use your active brand message in your marketing materials, consumer touch points, and sales presentations. This sentence should proclaim your business's promise and inspire prospects to hire you.

For example, a math tutoring service might have a brand message that says "Subtract difficulty from math tests in NYC." A gardening and lawn care service's tagline might be "Grow with us without wasting green."

Use the following five questions to help construct your one-liner:

1. What problem does your product or service solve?
2. What do customers hate about your competitors—and how will you be different?
3. What are your unique selling propositions?

4. What results do you provide customers?
5. What emotions will they experience after a job well done?

Write a clear and easy-to-read five- to eight-word sentence. Be sure to communicate the value your company can deliver. Avoid being overly clever, witty, or intellectual; you run the risk of customers not getting it, not caring to get it, or not liking what you have to say. Most importantly, don't just say something because it sounds cool. You don't have time or money to spout lofty ideals, nor do you possess the ability to shift pop culture in your favor with a multimillion-dollar ad campaign. You need your one-liner to spur business activity, attract interested prospects and produce revenue—*now.*

The next thing you'll need to do is match the appropriate promotion with your one-liner. Think of your promotion as an incentive meant to catch consumers' eyes and support the promise you've issued in your one-liner with some kind of guarantee.

For example: The math tutoring service might back up the "Subtract difficulty from math tests in NYC" message with a money-back grade improvement guarantee. The gardening and lawn care service's tagline of "Grow with us without wasting green" could be verified with an offer to plant a free tree or flower garden with their clients' first purchase.

Carefully determine how you will guarantee the promise you make in your one-liner. Since longevity is vital to your promotion, the offer should have staying power, versatility, and be catchy enough for consumers to easily remember when they want to spread the word about your company.

Make certain that your active brand message is a functional, revenue-generating marketing tool—not an exercise in creativity. Say what you do, know what you do, do what you say. Relate to the needs of the maximum number of people in your niche marketplace. Remember, any business can claim to be the best. Those who back up those statements with action, service, and concrete assurances truly *are* the best.

Diversify your brand message into targeted marketing messages. Saturating every channel at your disposal with the same exact marketing message isn't just lazy; it's insulting. Assuming that a Facebook fan and a general passerby are the same type of consumer because they both use some form of social media is like saying that a football fan and a hockey fan are the same because they both like sports.

In marketing, one size does not fit all—ever. The marketing message for a prospect typing your keywords into Google should be completely different in tone and approach than the one you'll use for flyers that you hand out on a street corner. Just because your niche marketplace is filled with multiple groups of like-minded individuals doesn't mean that all of them will interact with your marketing experience the same way, at the same time, or with the same intentions.

Before you commit to a marketing tactic, try to figure out how, when, and why prospects will interact, react, and connect with its content. Take everything into consideration—from the physical tool itself, to the actual location where the message will be delivered, to the actions that prospect will exercise, to the recipients themselves—before spending a *single* dollar or minute on any marketing tactic. Although it's important to maintain a uniform brand message, it's also vital to tailor your message and supportive offers to your specific targets' and distribution channels' needs. The better you are at attracting and pursuing your niche audiences—with the right messages delivered through the right channels—the higher your sales conversion rates will be.

Get the right tool for the job. Just as your marketing messages need to be customized, so do the distribution channels you use to send it. Consider all available options when determining the best tool for getting the job done. If your goal is to convert mothers walking down your local boulevard into impulse purchasers, then hiring a clown to make balloons for kids and handout coupons might do the trick. If you find the need to call passive community members into action, putting door hangers on their front doors might be the way to go.

Let your brand message determine the appropriate channels, and the channels inform your decisions about which marketing messages and tactics to use.

Think revenue, not brand marketing. If you assume that your logo, brand name, and contact information will form *any* kind of impression in your prospects' minds, you are naïve. There is absolutely no excuse for you to do "brand marketing" just to get the word out about your company name. A cool brand image or eye-catching design work means nothing unless it achieves something—a sale, a referral, or lead information.

Whether you create flyers, online ads, or brochures, you need to determine the purpose of the marketing materials you produce to ensure the best chance of producing your intended results. Each asset should have an objective and a goal, and each component— from headline and copy text to point of distribution—should be constructed with accomplishing those objectives and goals in mind.

For instance, the objective of a printed flyer for a dog-walking company might be to quickly alert dog lovers in local dog parks about its existence, and get prospects to share their contact information on the spot for future dog-walking services. Keeping this purpose in mind, it might be most effective to create and distribute a smaller, business card–sized flyer that touts the company's brand message, basic service information, and a special offer for a free dog treat for the card's recipient if they provide their contact information on the spot.

Consider the following five questions when developing each marketing tactic:

1. Does the marketing message take advantage of the deliverable as well as the intended distribution channel?
2. Does it properly represent your active brand message?
3. Does it offer multiple forms of contact information?
4. Is the presentation up to your standards?
5. Is everything about the tactic geared to the intended objective?

I can't tell you whether it's best for your business to send out mailings, spearhead e-mail campaigns, buy Google Ads, put door hangers on residential buildings, or do all of the above. After all, I'm not the expert in your niche marketplace; you are. What I *can* tell you is that no matter what tactics, channels, or deliverables you choose, your methodology will be the same.

Don't just market for the sake of marketing; market for *results*. Your marketing messages need to draw attention, provide context, and encourage consumers to interact with your brand immediately. Have specific reasons and set goals for spearheading an initiative—not because you feel you "have to market"—to make every second and dollar spent on marketing count.

Call to action, not inaction. Getting someone to pay attention to your marketing message isn't enough for it to be deemed a success. In fact, garnering attention without generating a single lead or sale as a result is nothing short of failure. You had a potential customer—and he slipped through your fingers.

Without the appropriate calls to action in your messages, all of your hard work in gaining a prospect's attention will be for nothing—and your newfound brand exposure will be rendered worthless. To that end, your messages must inspire action and participation.

To be effective, everything you do, say, and produce must encourage leads to contact your company, submit their info, make an immediate purchase, or refer others to your service, product, or offer. Anything else is a waste of time and money.

When you devise your call-to-action messaging and modes of communication, do all of the thinking *for* your prospect. Envision the entire exchange that she will have with your marketing messages—from the means by which the message will attract her attention, to how she'll consume the message, to the tools needed to enable a connection between her and your brand. Keep the her's mood and the activity in which she is likely engaged before, during, and after her encounter consistent with your message.

After careful consideration, determine how you can make your service relevant to her life in that moment. Think of ways to sweeten the deal; perhaps a free ice-cold lemonade on a hot day will get some foot traffic to your "Burger Boogle" stand. Maybe offering a free, relevant white paper or how-to guide on your Web site in exchange for a lead's contact information will generate sign-ups.

Give your leads a reason to contact you. Find the sweet spot between creativity, marketing messages, and special offers to trigger a response.

Do what it takes to get noticed. How many advertisements do you see in a day? Probably hundreds, if not thousands—if not tens of thousands. Yet how many do you *remember*? It is likely that you remember few, if any at all. Now here's the really challenging question: How will you avoid creating one of those insignificant marketing moments that you encounter and subsequently forget every day?

You don't need to spend much money to stand out. Nor do you need some overpriced marketing firm to create a massive campaign. Instead, you need to focus on smaller moments that add up to one big success.

A home-improvement company I know of achieved great success with funny T-shirts that read, "Got wood? I'll nail it!"— a short brand message, phone number, and e-mail address followed this humorous headline. The tactic was highly effective because it was inexpensive, it struck up conversations, and it turned a simple shirt into a lead-generating mechanism.

Play to your consumer's senses. Trigger their emotions to form connections and get responses. Put your brand out there in a fun, experiential, or shocking way to generate genuine interest and intrigue. Offer the unexpected or pair the absurd with the ordinary. Many people shy away from accepting handouts on street corners. However, if a Web-design firm hired a flyer distributor to stand on a street corner yelling about how much people should hate flyer distributors—while handing out a flyer that read, "Don't you hate when people hand you flyers like this?" along with a relevant offer that tied into the message, then the message's impact would be much stronger and offer a greater chance of success.

Content is king, but creativity is queen. The package in which your marketing message comes in is often just as important as the message itself. Anytime your name, logo, or other branded materials go out into the world, they are representing your entire brand. Ugly designs and grammar-inhibited phrases can change prospects into haters and skeptics in less than three seconds. A powerful message that is supported by a great offer and quality service can easily be diluted by a design that looks like a color blind kindergartner sketched it with a crayon.

Know how to wow. Make your marketing materials aesthetically appealing. Be conscious of your brand's design work. Competitors with better-designed tactics will win every time. Don't feel the urge to overdesign everything you produce either. This often leads to the same reaction as underdesigned work. If you don't have a creative bone in your body, be a tasteful minimalist.

Make sure that the design of your marketing package sets the right tone, feel, and level of professionalism you would expect from a trusted brand. If you think it looks unprofessional, scrap it until you create something that works.

Create Top-Quality Marketing Campaigns That Don't Break the Bank

Who needs a marketing director or creative department? By using low-cost tech products, inexpensive Web services, and crowd-sourcing marketplaces—where you can hire several hundred creative people for the price of one—your start-up can produce high-end marketing campaigns for little money. Here are 11 of my favorite products and online services that will help you produce and execute your marketing campaigns on the cheap.

1. **99designs.com** enables you to sponsor design and creative media competitions online where tens of thousands of creative freelancers compete to win cash prizes—and *you* only pay for the winning designs. Cost: Varies.

2. **OvernightPrints.com** is an online short-run printing company that lets you print almost any type of high-quality, full-color marketing collateral on the cheap. Cost: Varies.

3. **Voices.com** lets you choose a spokesperson for your videos and audio spots from tens of thousands of professional voice-over talents. Cost: Varies.

4. **Flickr Creative Commons** (flickr.com) is a user-generated photo repository that lets you select from millions of photos and use them royalty-free for your marketing materials. Cost: Free.

5. **iContact.com** is an e-mail marketing service that allows you to easily manage intuitive e-mail marketing campaigns to your opt-in subscribers. Cost: Free to $240 per month.

6. **Flip Video Camcorders** are handheld devices capable of shooting standard or high-definition videos for your Web sites and social media networks. Cost: Starting at $99.99.

7. **Qik.com** is a mobile video service that lets you record and share live or prerecorded videos instantly from your mobile phone. Cost: Free to $49.99 per phone per month.

8. **JayCut.com** is Web-based video editing program that lets you professionally edit your media anywhere, anytime on any computer. Cost: Free to varies.

9. **Involver.com** is an app company that specializes in professional, dynamic applications such as video players, RSS feeds, polls, slideshows, and coupon modules for Facebook Fan Pages. Cost: Free to varies.

10. **Picnik.com** is an online photo-editing program that enables you to import files from your computer or social media networks and add effects and text. Cost: Free to $24.95 per year.

11. **Google AdWords** is one of the Internet's most prominent ad-buying platforms and enables you to bid on and buy ads globally on Google as well as various other mediums, including television. Cost: Varies.

Encourage repeat business with a finishing touch. Even though a customer might have paid you for your service, that doesn't mean that your marketing job is over quite yet. Nothing says thank you more than a small, unexpected gesture. There isn't much that's better for your business than taking advantage of the opportune moment when your client is at his most satisfied state with your service to solidify life-long loyalty, encourage the spread of word-of-mouth, and engage the satisfied customer with an incentive to use your services again in the future.

For example, Sizzle It!, offers a year's supply of free coffee with a customer's first purchase. The coffee arrives at the client's office along with a personalized thank-you note, a referral offer, and free coffee mug with Sizzle It!'s logo, marketing message, and contact information. This gift keeps our brand relevant by getting our marketing real estate in a place where it can serve as a potential conversation starter among coworkers.

Who wouldn't be curious to know why a coworker received free coffee for a year from a "video company?"

You have one shot to get this right—so don't mess it up. Simply handing someone crappy marketing materials will put a bad taste in his mouth at the worst possible moment. Your finishing touch must provide your customer with real, tangible value. It also needs to be as purposeful for your brand as it is useful and thoughtful to your client. If you're going to give something away, make sure it serves a dual purpose: to thank the customer and to call him back into action. Giving away pens and pads is all well and good, but if you fail to make them into effective selling tools by only including your logo and contact information, you're missing out on a valuable opportunity.

Don't pass up the chance to ingrain your brand in your customer's mind and turn them into a lead generator or a repeat customer. One happy client can pay off 10 times over.

THINK GUERRILLA, NOT GODZILLA

As you're well aware by now, you don't exactly have an unlimited checkbook to spend on marketing and advertising, which is all the more reason to make sure that everything you do or produce performs at the top of its game. To be a successful start-up marketer, you need to produce results on the cheap and become an 800-pound *guerrilla*. This is why it's important that you learn to turn any circumstance or space into an effective marketing moment for your brand—one that converts eyeballs into cash.

Don't rely on expensive ads. I love listening to ad salespeople pitch me case studies and statistics. Often these facts and figures are anything but the norm or what can be expected. Those case study subjects who broke the mold didn't just magically place their ads into a newspaper or e-blast and automatically get that response; they found a way to maximize the medium by inserting the right message content and creativity. Whether you decide that your brand and marketing messages will be most effective in churches or bars, your challenge isn't to determine *how much* it will cost you to get your messages there, but rather how you can get them there with minimal, if any, up-front costs.

Find the best ways to control and disseminate your own brand and marketing messages while taking advantage of the audiences and eyeballs advertisers pay big bucks to target. Instead of taking out a newspaper ad, you might decide to drop neighborhood-specific flyers with special offers into your neighbors' mailboxes. If an event sponsorship is too steep, you might consider attending as a guest, mingling, and then handing out business cards and marketing materials to attendees.

Limited cash demands that you come up with smart guerrilla marketing tactics. Hosting contests, giving away free product samples and gift certificates, wearing T-shirts with catchy marketing messages, adding special offers in your e-mail signature, producing online videos, and conducting local publicity stunts are examples of tactics that can yield high returns on investment for little up-front capital. Look for ways to transform ordinary objects, situations, or cheap materials into effective marketing tools that produce results.

You're an expert (just ask you)! As the creator of your service, *you* know that you offer your niche marketplace valuable insight and advice. However, simply proclaiming that you are an expert will get you nowhere. It's not enough to just shamelessly pimp your own service; you also need to become a leading authority for your target customers.

Devise a moniker for which you want to be known for marketing and public relations purposes. Perhaps you want to be known as "The Green Dad" with an expertise in outdoor family activities in order to front your sports adventure travel company. To put a face to your gluten-free baking company, you may want others to label you as "The Gluten Free Cooking Queen" whose passion is to teach others to create great quality baked goods without the gluten.

Authenticity builds credibility. Don't speak down to your customers; relate to them. Tell the story of how your service was founded. What problems did you encounter? How did you solve them? Give people a reason to listen to you by offering value to their lives with relevant and targeted information. Offer a fresh perspective in your market. Take a stand, be controversial, and pick a side on issues that are important to your niche marketplace.

Once you've perfected your message, syndicate your way to success by distributing content through the "expert real estate"—blogs, forums, press releases, newsletters, Web video, and podcasts—in your niche marketplace. Join and lead local industry groups or associations. Find guest blogging opportunities by reaching out to like-minded Web sites and offering your services at no charge. Build online communities centered on your expertise. Remember, no one knows your marketplace better than you.

Become a Syndicated Media Personality and Expert

You don't need to be a pundit on a major TV network or a celebrity to attract notoriety, create a buzz, and establish expertise. In fact, as long as you've got a valuable message and supportive content, you can transform yourself into a relevant niche expert in a matter of minutes.

But remember—tools alone won't draw crowds or attention. Everyone, including your competition, has access to these resources. When combined with the right message, personality-driven content, consistency, and a multichannel marketing approach, these 11 distribution channels can form a powerful platform from which to build your brand expertise and maximize your SEO.

1. **Justin.tv or UStream.tv** allow you to produce your own TV program or video tutorial. Forget big budgets, camera crews, or expensive equipment. With these services, all you need is a webcam or any other compatible video camera to host a live video show in seconds. Cost: Free.

2. **Blip.tv** enables you to instantly syndicate your videos to various video-sharing sites, such as YouTube, AOL, Vimeo, iTunes, and many more. Cost: Free to $8 per month.

3. **Connect with consumers** by signing up for free user accounts on all relevant social networks, such as Facebook, Ning, and LinkedIn. Use profile spaces to position your message, market your service, distribute insights to fans, and connect with prospects, consumers, and enthusiasts. Cost: Free.

4. **Start a blog** providing relevant tips, tricks, and advice to readers; connect it with your Web site, and send links to prospects and customers regularly. Don't use your blog for aggressive selling; be informative and useful, and inject the occasional *passive* sales offer. Your blog must be used as a tool, not a hobby, in order for it to effective. A blog that is dormant for long periods of time will hurt you more than help you; it either shows readers that you really don't have much to say or that you don't really care enough about them to be consistent. Make a schedule, make it public, and stick to it. Blogger, WordPress, and Tumblr all offer free blog hosting. Cost: Free.

5. **Ping.fm** is a free online service that instantly syndicates your messages, videos, photos, and media content to almost

(continued)

(*continued*)

every social network, blogging site, media-sharing site, and micro-blogging site across the Internet. Cost: Free.

6. **BlogTalkRadio.com** enables you to become the host of a syndicated radio show and podcast. You don't need a big-time studio to get your voice on the airwaves. Use this platform to interview guests and stream your message over the Web. iTunes, PodcastAlley.com, and Podcast.com are also free distribution services to syndicate your message to a wider online audience. Cost: Free to $199 per month.

7. **TokBox.com** is a Web-based tool that enables you to host live lectures, seminars, and video chats with up to 200 people, schedule and invite people in advance, and share presentations and documents. Cost: Free to varies.

8. **PRWeb.com** can be a powerful distribution channel for your message. PR Web is not a free or inexpensive service, but it is the absolute authority in distributing press releases to members of the press and online news outlets. Cost: Varies.

9. **Hootsuite.com** links to your Twitter accounts to schedule tweets, tweet RSS feeds, and shorten elongated URLs. You may also want to consider other popular micro-blogging sites Tumblr and Posterous, in addition to Twitter. Cost: Free.

10. **Get syndicated** by posting your expert content across the Internet. The more places your content shows up on the Web, the more opportunities there will be for you to attract new followers to your social media streams, improve your SEO, and sell new clients on your product or service. There are hundreds of Web sites where you can blog and post content, but I highly recommend Facebook Notes, EzineArticles.com, IdeaMarketers.com, EvanCarmichael.com, GoArticles.com, and Scribd.com. Cost: Free.

11. **HelpAReporter.com** is a social media service that connects journalists with sources for their news stories. Cost: Free.

Pay off referrers. For the right price, anyone's time and energy can be bought—even if that person isn't someone who would directly benefit from using your product or service.

If you only market with members of your niche marketplace in mind, you'll be missing out on the millions of others who are acquainted with those in your target market. The person who sees your marketing message might not need your products—but there's a pretty good chance she either knows or will meet several people along the way who fit the bill.

Buy people off to get your brand message to the right leads, and not just your already-happy customers—everyone and anyone. Although offering a potential business referrer a gift certificate to use your services might be a lost cause, a more generic proposal—such as referral gift cards for popular consumer products or services—just might do the trick.

Sizzle It! offers a free breakfast for a person's entire office in exchange for any referral that converts into a successful sale. This spreads the word about our company even further.

Find generic, brand-appropriate incentives to turn regular Janes and Joes into salespeople and brand ambassadors. Feed their impulses for your gain. Remember to have a signed agreement or money in the bank to show for the free stuff you're giving away before you express your gratitude.

You're the worst person to say you're the best. As I mentioned earlier, claiming to be the best will give you slightly more credibility than a prison inmate. Scrap the self-aggrandizing garbage in favor of a better approach: mainly, employing the services of the best sales team available to you to attract new customers: your current customers.

After every successful transaction, ask your happy clients for a testimonial detailing their experiences and recommending your service to others. Get these accounts in both video and audio whenever possible, because this media will play a vital role in your offline and online marketing efforts. Place these testimonials everywhere you can post them—from your Web site to your social media profiles.

Turn your customers into mouthpieces and offer prospects someone with whom they can relate. Use your clients' images, titles, and words to sell new clients on your value.

It's not personal; it's business marketing. Publicly challenging your competition by flaunting their weaknesses is a great way to overtly differentiate your business and tout its strengths.

React to competitor missteps, broken promises, or underperformance with impunity. If a competitor raises prices, you might push out a series of marketing messages that show customers how much they could save by choosing your company instead. If they have a record of poor customer service, you might decide to build a series of marketing messages around one of their former customer's testimonials. For every big story in the press about a competitor's mistake, celebrate by providing a special offer to their disenfranchised customers.

Flex some marketplace muscle. Latch on to your competitor's brand recognition to elevate your own.

However, remember to use discretion when taking your competitors to task. Don't just decide to knock the competition without rhyme or reason. Take a strong stand, but make sure to base that stand on something valid. The intention of this exercise shouldn't be to come off as a whining baby who's bitter because his company is in second place. It's a power move with the sole purpose of pointing out to customers why their dollar is better spent with you than the other guy. Focus on facts, not opinions, and maintain a high level of professionalism. Keep your efforts focused on taking market share away from competitors based on their actions and inactions with respect to their customers. Say why you're a better option—don't just proclaim that they suck.

Under no circumstance should you be libelous or untruthful when referring to your competitors. There are real legal ramifications for making fraudulent statements.

However, give competitors a reason to notice and respond to you, and don't let up on your assault. Should they make the mistake of acknowledging your existence, they'll be doing you a big favor by putting you on the map to a whole new world of consumers—and openly recognizing you as an equal. Doing so will provide your business with legitimacy and lend you credibility—ammunition you can use to continue your conquest of more market share.

Most importantly, back up *everything* you say with action and pristine service. If you mess up by overpromising or underdelivering, your competitors will be happy to never let you or your prospects forget it.

Know how to react so you can attract. If you're a proficient reaction marketer, you're able to link your brand and marketing messages to any current event or pop culture trend—no matter how absurd the connection—and make it work. Many businesses have used recession, weather, and even home runs hit by major league ball players to market special offers to customers and generate sales.

Reaction marketing also helps your business get noticed in the press, because many publications—print and online—often seek out quirky stories for holidays and special occasions. For example, one of my clients—a bar and restaurant in New York City—jumped onboard the hoopla over Mattel's celebration of Barbie's 50th Anniversary by creating and hosting an event called, Barbie's Birthday Beauty Pageant Blow Out. Barbie enthusiasts from all over NYC came out to compete in a runway-style competition as their favorite Barbie. Not only did this event generate revenue on an off-night, it also garnered weeks' worth of press and media coverage—from blogs to local television coverage to national newspaper stories.

Put yourself in a position to tie your brand and marketing messages to the right big stories. Take advantage of mood shifts and attention grabbers in the market as they come. Don't try to start trends—that's way too expensive an endeavor. Instead, hop aboard preexisting ones or those on the break. Know what's going on in the news and popular culture. Larger competitors might be slower to act due to their by-committee decision-making style, but you can react to the outside world instantly. Always adhere to your brand message, but make sure that you remain fresh, creative, and fun to take advantage of what's hot and keep your brand relevant.

How to Be Your Own PR Firm without Spending $10k a Month

PR firms charge ridiculous fees—sometimes as high as tens of thousands of dollars per month. Clearly, your start-up can't afford that, but that doesn't mean you can't do the same thing they do. In fact, many PR firms use their junior account managers and entry-level employees to handle actual press outreach—many of whom are no more qualified to handle PR campaigns than you are!

Here are 12 tips on how to engage the media, get your story in journalists' hands, and gain notoriety for your business.

1. **Never *just* pitch your company.** Pitch a reporter about the launch of your homemade ice-cream, and you'll be lucky to even get a rejection e-mail. Pitch the launch of your business *along with* a branded promotion attached—say, a "Free Ice Cream Day" that offers everyone in the community a free scoop—then you might have a shot. Members of the media won't care about your business unless they see a story angle that benefits their readers or viewers. Do your homework and focus your pitch on the amazing, unique

things they care about. And *always* support your pitch with your expertise and credentials.

2. **Insert yourself into big stories.** The media will only care about writing a feature exclusively about your start-up if it's acquired for billions, hits an incredible milestone directly relevant to their audiences, or is sued by a conglomerate. However, you don't need to *be* the big story to find ways to insert yourself into one as an expert source. Use Google Trends to find out what's popular and determine creative ways to tie your brand into trending topics.

3. **If it bleeds it leads.** In most cases, editorial and advertising divisions of publications and media outlets are similar to church and state. But without advertising, there can be no press outlet. In order to get advertising, a publication needs to attract an audience, which they often do by leading with stories to grab the eyeballs—that is, brutal murders or Lindsay Lohan on page one. Whether they admit it or not, most press outlets are about ratings first and *important* content second. You must spin your pitches to stir genuine emotional responses. If you don't spin a story aiming for page one, you probably won't end up on page 40.

4. **Find the right media outlets.** Visit book stores and newspaper stands and search free Web sites and online news aggregators like Blogpulse.com, Technorati.com, MondoTimes .com, Technorati.com, Alltop.com, and World-Newspapers .com. Use your brand language, keywords, and competitors' names to find the names and URLs of relevant media outlets covering your niche marketplace.

5. **Build a press list.** Many writers include their e-mail addresses in their social media profiles or in the bylines or footers of their articles or blogs. Most local news stations have a tip line and a news desk e-mail address readily accessible.

(*continued*)

(*continued*)

For those that don't, consider using these free and low-cost services to find the contact information for the appropriate reporters and journalists covering your niche marketplace's beat: Mastheads.org (Cost: Varies), EasyMediaList.org (Cost: Varies), and MediaonTwitter.com (Cost: Free).

6. **Fit the pitch to the outlet.** If your niche marketplace reads a certain magazine with content that doesn't quite fit with your brand message, find a way to give it the right spin. A junk removal service might benefit tremendously from a woman's fashion magazine if they find that their main customers are women. Perhaps the company could pitch a story about how to "turn junk into chic." Obviously, that's an extreme example, but you get the point. Originality has a funny way of turning pitches that shouldn't be stories into featured articles and news material.

7. **Tailor pitches to the right person.** Sending generic, boilerplate e-mails with press release attachments is how amateurs who *don't get it* pitch reporters. This method shows absolutely no respect for the person you are pitching. It just lets them know that you didn't put any thought into pitching them. I assure you they'll "return the favor" by adding your e-mail address to their spam filter. Read their columns and make your pitch relevant to that writer or editor and their publications.

8. **Know the publication schedule.** Different media outlets have different calendars. Blogs and local TV are likely daily, whereas certain magazines and newspaper features may be planned weeks or months in advance. In many cases, you'll be able to search online or contact your targeted outlet's advertising department to get their editorial calendar. This will help you see what types of stories the outlet will be publishing, and help you determine how far in advance you need to begin pitching.

9. **Write a killer subject line.** Whatever you do, do not write generic subject lines such as "hey" or "interesting story about a local business." Understand that most journalists and editors get hundreds—sometimes thousands—of e-mail pitches every day. To a local newspaper, a subject line such as "Joe's Catering Co. to host a BBQ competition to raise $100,000 for cancer research" will have a much better chance of getting attention than "Local company to host fund-raiser." "Hey." Put as much, if not more, time into your e-mail's subject line than the pitch itself.

10. **Timing is everything.** In my experience, the best days to send out pitches are Tuesday, Wednesday, or Thursday between the hours of 7:30 AM and 11 AM, or between 2 PM and 4 PM. I've found that most journalists consider Mondays as catch-up days, Fridays as "I can't wait for the weekend" days—and weekends as, well, weekends!

11. **Follow up *without* being a pain in the ass.** Every PR person has his or her own version of this routine, but I have found the most success in this follow-up schedule: After sending my initial inquiry, I wait two days. If I don't hear anything, I re-forward my previous e-mail with the words "Follow Up" in the beginning of the subject line instead of the "Fwd" and add a quick two liner about following up within the body of the e-mail. If still I don't hear anything after another 24 hours, I call once and leave a message. If I still don't hear anything, I call a few more times over the course of the following week without leaving a message until I get someone on the phone or I'm told I'm dead in the water. Whenever you leave messages, leave your phone number twice and your e-mail address twice—once spelled out—so that whoever's checking his or her messages quickly doesn't miss anything.

(continued)

(*continued*)

12. **Be ready to monetize your press mentions.** Your company's name in print or on local TV will mean nothing without an associated promotion to drive lead generation and, ultimately, sales. Make sure that your pitch includes a tailored offer and action message that turns eyeballs into cash. Keep your press links and clippings on your Web site, social media profiles, and applicable sales and marketing materials to elongate your press's revenue-generation potential.

Support the locals. Does your town have a favorite sports team? Are there major political or economic events affecting your area? Getting in sync with your community can put you on the map with local influencers and help you to build a loyal base of local customers.

If you live in a town hit hard by recession, perhaps you can offer a "blockbuster recession special." If the local little league team is on its way to the state championships, maybe you can donate a portion of your sales toward equipment, travel, or lodging expenses.

Become part of the fabric of your community. Tie your marketing efforts into your local community's activities and events. Do something that larger competitors can't: care about the little guy. Give back, but look for ways to get back as well. Remember, your goal shouldn't just be to be seen as a nice guy; you also have to concentrate on converting your fellow community members into loyal customers. Feel good about what you're doing, yes, but don't let your compassion guide you into blowing all of your time and available funds on being a do-gooder.

Scratch lots of people's backs. Consumers in your niche marketplace are also consumers of other like-minded businesses and service providers. Connecting with these other businesses can offer you direct lines of communication to even more consumers without the need to spend capital up-front.

Find partners that either benefit from similar clientele or that can enhance their bottom lines by offering a cross promotion to their consumer bases. For example, a florist might connect with caterers and wedding planners to offer them a percentage of sales generated from referrals. A house-cleaning service might consider a mutually beneficial package deal with a dry cleaner whose market also consists of affluent customers who like convenience.

Whether you build partnerships based on gross revenue shares or commissions, link up with complementary, noncompetitive service providers whose existing customers fall into your niche marketplace—and make their customers your customers.

Get real about social media marketing. I have news for you: People aren't going to magically flock to your Facebook Fan Page. Nor will you have 5,000,000 followers on Twitter—ever. And if you think social media is going to make your business an overnight success, think again. In reality, when you open up shop in the social media world, absolutely nothing will come out of it; not a single person will care about your profile except you.

Social media is meant to be used it as an amplifier, not a campaign unto itself. It's supplemental, not the whole ball of wax.

Failed social media campaigns are those that are too intensely focused on trying to get hoards of followers—instead of appealing to the enthusiasts and brand ambassadors who truly care about your brand, and are willing to spread the message. Whereas effective social media strategies support larger marketing objectives—and avoid becoming time-draining, life-consuming tasks.

Look to build and foster relationships online by providing valuable content in a voice with which your users can easily identify. Get to know your audience before you bombard them with wall posts and status updates. Tailor your brand's communications to each network; become aware of the language, phrases, and key terms of the social media platform you're working on before you engage its community. And whatever

The 9 Rules of Social Media Marketing

Like every other marketing tactic or channel, your social media initiatives must be focused and goal-oriented. Dedicating too much time, providing too little value, or having unrealistic expectations can turn any social media strategy into a bottomless pit that bares less fruit than a cactus in the Sahara. Here are 9 ways to avoid pointless social media marketing activities and produce results.

1. **Create valuable content.** This is an overly saturated tip—but that doesn't make it any less true. No one will listen if you simply talk about yourself or advertise your product. You have to build your following by offering insightful information. Let your content demonstrate what's great about you and your brand, and the value you can offer others.
2. **Choose dynamic media over text.** Opt to use dynamic content, such as images and videos, over text. These have a higher rate of going viral and attracting attention.
3. **Be social, but professional.** No one cares about what you eat or when you're going to the gym—unless you're a chef or a trainer. Likewise, don't talk *at* your fans and followers; talk *with* them. Don't preach from a mountaintop; be one of the gang. Have timely conversations instead of lectures.
4. **Be relevant to your niche marketplace.** Always stay one step ahead of your fans' and followers' needs and pain points. Lead your marketplace by offering solutions and advice that tackles the issues your followers face at present and will face tomorrow—not yesterday. Help users solve problems, gain access to important information, and connect with one another.
5. **Shout out fellow experts, fans, and content creators.** Share quality content from other content providers with your followers. Interview people or fellow experts who can provide value to your fans. Let content creators know

when you shouted them out in their Web site's comments section or via e-mail to get on their radar. Encourage users to join conversations and allow them to comment on your posts by integrating services such as Disqus (disqus.com) on your site (Cost: Free).

6. **Recruit a social media nation.** Add a social media component to your offering that encourages users to create and share viral media about your product or service and its results with their social networks and friends. For example, an event-planning business might host mobile photo contests at their events, or a fitness company might offer discounts to customers who post their weekly weight losses and toning results on Facebook.

7. **Always get fans and followers back to your site.** Don't help Facebook and Twitter make more money! They don't care about you—so don't care about them! At the end of the day, hoards of fans and followers mean nothing unless they visit your site, offer you their contact information, convert into consumers, and generate immediate revenue.

8. **Track everything, and systemize your social media marketing.** Don't just tweet for the sake of tweeting; tweet to drive Web traffic and consumer engagement. Use tools such as Google Analytics, Bit.ly, and HootSuite.com to analyze exactly what is bringing people to your Web site. Your travel agency might find that Monday is a great day to launch polls to determine the "Trip of the Week." Wednesday may be the best day to pick the winning vacation and post an online video about it, while Thursday is the best day to offer a last-minute trip deal to your followers. Figure out what works, and scrap what doesn't. Use what you learn to create a social media content calendar and build an effective production and sharing schedule.

(continued)

(*continued*)

9. **Use competitors' social media against them.** Subscribe to all of your competitor's social media feeds to stay informed about their promotions and posts. Anytime they point out their new features or services, find ways to weaken their positions in your market. They may tout a "new" service in a press release, but you've had a similar service for months. Although they might talk about a new lower price, your price is still lower. Take advantage of any weakness and share it with the social media world.

you do, do not spam users with excessive direct messages or marketing speak.

Rally prospects behind a cause. Linking yourself to a charity, relief effort, or local fund-raiser can win over big followings while simultaneously doing some good. Your efforts may include giving a percentage of sales away to a nonprofit organization, or helping those in need by offering your time or services.

Choose a cause that not only makes you feel good, but also fits your brand image and matches your niche market profile. A dog-walking service that works with an animal hospital makes sense, whereas a cleaning service teamed up with an animal hospital might not. Whatever cause you support, be sure to follow through with the goals you set forth. Speak to members of your charity and see how you can tie into its community and vice versa. Clearly state your intended contributions in all of your applicable marketing materials and communications.

I'm warning you, though: using cause-marketing just to further your agenda will come back to bite you in the ass later. Loyalists and enthusiasts will hunt your brand down and make your life miserable if they find out you're doing wrong by their mission. So feel good while generating profits, not pickets.

CONCLUSION

BE AFRAID. BE VERY AFRAID.

So, how do you feel? Pumped? Excited? Empowered? Think you have what it takes to make it on your own two feet? Are you salivating at the opportunity to duke it out with the titans for market share? Counting down the minutes until you tell your boss where he can shove his TPS reports?

Well, good, but that's not enough. Now comes the hard part: Actually *doing* it.

This is the moment of truth—the moment when you decide to get in the game or remain on the sidelines. Reading this book to deconstruct and rebuild yourself was a great first step, but it was just that: a first step. The trick now is to make sure it wasn't your last step.

I won't lie to you. It will take *a lot* of hard work to maintain your enthusiasm, persistence, and passion for your entrepreneurial ambitions. It will take even more work and discipline to stick with it for more than just a few days or weeks. But at the end of the day, all that matters is your answer to this question: Do you want to be an employee—or seek employment—to benefit others—or be self-employed to benefit yourself?

If you find that you're not up for the challenge, just do what most start-up book readers do: Nothing. Put down this book, forget everything I've taught you, and continue your life as it exists today. Hide behind excuses like "It's too hard," "I don't have enough money to get started," or "I'll get started one day"—and go on collecting paychecks or searching for a "real" job.

There will only be a beginning if you choose for there to be one. No one else will start your business for you, or force you to keep your promises to yourself. Every day that you fail to take immediate actions to materialize your entrepreneurial goal is just one more day you'll remain a slave to the "real" job—whether you have one or not.

Bottom line: If you want to be an entrepreneur, don't just talk about doing it; *do* it. If you want more out of this life, fight for it. If you crave freedom and fulfillment, chase after it with your full mind and body. If you yearn to snub the antiquated social norm, get off your ass and make it happen!

Am I rooting against you? No. I *hope* you go on to build the business of your dreams and credit this book as one of the reasons for your success. However, I'd be doing you a disservice if after all of this, I gave you an undeserved pat on the back and congratulated you just because you can read at an eighth grade level.

So what are you waiting for?

Start now.

Not tomorrow. Not next week. Right now.

Be part of the select few who will actually take this moment to change his or her life and get out of the system that is strangling your future before it's too late.

I leave you with these parting words of inspiration that a fellow entrepreneur once told me: Be afraid. Be very afraid.

Be afraid to have never failed.

Be afraid of living with regrets for the rest of your life.

Be afraid of letting others dictate what you should be afraid of.

Be afraid of putting other people before yourself, never earning what you're worth, or losing your entire livelihood in an instant without any say in the matter.

Be afraid of waking up at 50 and realizing that your career has been nothing more than a patchwork of dead-end "real" jobs with nothing to show for it.

Finally, be afraid to live out the rest of your life as a mere dreamer rather than a doer who dreams up what's next.

Reading time is now over. You've got lots to do—and you're already behind.

Help Spread the Word About the "Never Get a 'Real' Job" Movement

Stay in the know: Follow me on Twitter @askgerber and friend me on Facebook at facebook.com/scottgerber. Join the *Never Get a "Real" Job* community at NeverGetARealJob.com where you can make the pledge to never get a "real" job, watch my *Ask Gerber* Web show, get regularly updated tips and tricks from top young entrepreneurs, and much more!

Index

HOW TO SAVE THOUSANDS OF DOLLARS
ON START-UP EXPENSES THANKS TO
NEVER GET A "REAL" JOB

As a thank-you for purchasing *Never Get a "Real" Job* and committing yourself to dumping your boss, tearing up your résumés, and starting a *real* business, my friends—some of today's top small business service providers—and I have assembled a series of exclusive NGARJ offers, freebies, and discounts for you to help get your start-up on its feet—on the cheap.

Sure, I could have offered you some BS special report or free video seminar meant to bolster and sell my personality brand, but—as you no doubt know by now—I'd rather get something practical in your hands that will help you to move your business forward and get your start-up on the path to generating immediate revenue.

Here's how you can claim your NGARJ special offers:

Step One:
Go to this URL: www.NeverGetARealJob.com/purchased

Step Two:
You'll be asked to identify certain words on specific pages to verify your purchase.

Step Three:

You'll be given instructions about how to redeem each of the following company's coupon codes, discounts, and special offers:

99designs	oDesk
AdRoll.com	Plum Choice
Animoto	PollDaddy.com
Blog Talk Radio	PR Web
Box.net	RescueTime
DimDim	Right Signature
DocStoc	Setster
Efax	ShoeBoxed
EmailStationery.com	Shopify
Flowtown.com	SitePal
FreshBooks	SlideRocket
Get Satisfaction	Urban Interns
Grasshopper	UserVoice
Google AdWords	Voices.com
iContact	Weebly
MoFuse	Wufoo
Moo	

Now get to work and make use of this stuff!

All the best along your journey,

Scott

P.S. I'm always available to spread the *Never Get a "Real" Job* mission. Find out more information about booking me for speaking engagements and panels at NeverGetARealJob.com.